STEAM ON THE SHED

By the same author

MAIN LINE ALBUM
NARROW GAUGE ALBUM
ON THE NARROW GAUGE
BRANCH LINE ALBUM (TWO VOLUMES)
FESTINIOG RAILWAY REVIVAL
TRALEE AND DINGLE RAILWAY
RAILWAY ANTHOLOGY
STEAM IN EUROPE

with John Adams
RAILWAY ROUNDABOUT BOOK
RAILWAY PICTURE GALLERY

with Sir Peter Allen
ROUND THE WORLD ON THE NARROW GAUGE
NARROW GAUGE RAILWAYS OF EUROPE

with L. T. C. Rolt
LINES OF CHARACTER

STEAM ON THE SHED

P. B. Whitehouse OBE, ARPS, FRSA

LONDON

IAN ALLAN

First published 1969

SBN 7110 0080–8

*Published by Ian Allan Ltd., Shepperton, Surrey and printed in
the United Kingdom by R. J. Acford Ltd., Chichester, Sussex*

Acknowledgements

A book which contains as many pictures as this does mean that its author owes a great deal to the large number of people who have made this possible. These naturally include the Railway authorities whose permission to visit the various depots has been so kindly given; individual railwaymen who have moved engines to more photographic positions, and those who have paused a while during their working day to impart information and give friendly advice. One of the great pleasures of producing a book on railways is the way in which one is given so much help so readily in almost every country one visits. This may seem normal enough here in England, but elsewhere the railway photographer is sometimes viewed with just a little suspicion and explanations must be given well in advance to the authorities, but in the end all is generally well. I would like to thank the railway administrations of all the countries in Europe and the New World who have made this book possible—the PROs of the old Big Four railways here in the UK and their later successors in the BR regions—starting with D. S. Barrie, now a Region General Manager but one time PRO to the Railway Executive—he and his colleagues are owed much by we railway photographers. Then come other Railway friends who have done much to help—M Canioni of French Railways, Edip Sirmem of the Turkish State Railways, Igor Ahvanahti of Finnish Railways, the Community of Yugoslav Railways, and last but not least an unknown Senior Official of the Hungarian State Railways at Budapest West who made photography possible when we thought that all was lost.

My two friends John Adams and John Snell have once more given me valuable assistance, the former by providing the means of making prints from my negatives, and the latter by reading through, correcting and checking the text, and I am deeply grateful to them. Most of the photographs have come from my own cameras—ranging from an old Kodak No 1A folding, to a Rolleiflex, but there are also some from my collection of A.W. Croughton's negatives—he did a grand job and history is in his debt. This book has been a family affair—my wife has spent hours typing the manuscript and my son Michael has contributed to the photographic contents; maybe this has been the most satisfying part of all.

Contents

Introduction

On Thursday, August 1, 1968, I climbed up on to the footplate of an ex-LMS Stanier Black Five at Carnforth shed, and we set off to pick up a trip freight to Morecambe. At first glance there may seem to be nothing unusual about this, but in fact it was a somewhat emotional experience, for there were then but two days of regular work left for the steam engines of British Rail, and Carnforth was one of the last three depots to remain open.

It is partly to commemorate that now completed era that the photographs on the following pages have been gathered together, for the 'shed' or 'depot' was the steam engine's home, and thousand upon thousand of enthusiasts have, through the courtesy of the Railway Authorities, visited them there. Some have gone to record numbers for collections, others to photograph, and many just to look and drink in the atmosphere of steam; these people have come from all walks of life—postmen and prelates, amateurs and professional railwaymen, and it is the magic of the steam engine which has drawn them all.

Now, in 1969, apart from those lines and locomotives which have been preserved, there is no steam here in England. The last steam engine of all, one of Riddles' Britannias—*Oliver Cromwell*—was the final example, has now gone 'on shed', preserved on behalf of BR by Alan Bloom at Diss in Norfolk. In Europe a similar pattern is evolving and the next decade will see the virtual extinction of motive power on the Stephenson principle. But there is still time, for most countries in Europe have something left to show—the French Pacifics may have gone from Calais, but as yet the American- and Canadian-built 141 Rs remain; there is no narrow gauge in Belgrade, but its shed still has a great deal of steam in among the American diesels; and although Austria is largely electrified, the 'Giesl machines' can be found on both standard and narrow gauges. Those who are responsible for caring for motive power, the depot masters, even today have a nostalgia for this piece of yesterday, which has done so much to advance civilisation as we know it, and the steam shed has not yet become a complete anachronism.

The photographs in this book show something of the steam engine at home over a period of nearly half a century—from the peak of its achievement to its ultimate decline here in England. I hope that they will bring joy to those who have known this time and those who have seen railways when they really were a nationally recognised form of public transport. To those who have not known the days which were sometimes good, may this historical record give them heart to seek out that which is left—it is still worth it.

P.B.W.

Engines of the 'Twenties and 'Thirties

It is surprising just how pampered railway enthusiasts have become during the past twenty years or so. There has been a plethora of books on railway subjects; visits to depots, special trains, lectures and film shows have been arranged almost at the drop of a hat and programmes on railways have even appeared on television. How different in so many ways to the scene say forty years ago. Then it was only the minority who was lucky enough to actually *visit* a shed. Most engines were seen from the lineside or from station platforms, and to discover where an engine was actually allocated was a gargantuan task unless you asked its driver in person or lived across the way from its shed.

But there were some groups of pioneer spirits. Without doubt the greatest of these were the Stephenson Locomotive Society, a learned body who did not take to the idea of shed visits just to see engines too kindly, and the newly-formed Railway Correspondence and Travel Society, which celebrated its 40th anniversary in 1968. This was founded in Cheltenham, to cater for the ordinary enthusiast: among its early members was one now General Manager of a BR Region. It was the RCTS (and its later imitators) who made sure that not only did we humble enthusiasts have the opportunity of going on organised visits to depots but also provided us at least once a year, by courtesy of the main line companies concerned, detailed locomotive allocation booklets.

The 40th anniversary issue of the 'Railway Observer', the journal of the RCTS, recalls typical examples of items of interest in its first issue of May 1928 when it was called 'The Railway News'. One concerned Rugby LMS depot whose allocation of ninety-six locomotives on April 10, 1928 included forty passenger and fifty-six freight and shunting locomotives. Apart from the then new Royal Scots. of which there were four, the passenger engines were all products of the 'Premier Line': Claughtons, Princes, Georges, Precursors and even a Renown, 5158 *Temeraire*, and Jumbo 5012 *John Ramsbottom*. On the freight side thirty LNWR 0-8-0s formed the largest group and only six engines are listed from other sources, three Midland 4F 0-6-0s and three 0-6-0 tanks. A list of passenger engines allocated to Midland sheds was also appended and this was printed in full. This was most welcome information to enthusiasts living in the South, as it represented a glimpse of far off and practically unobtainable objectives. This was the happy beginning of organised railway enthusiasm and there can be no doubt that the trouble taken by the two pioneer societies to ensure that their affairs have been conducted in a responsible way has led to the privileges afforded to us all today. So interest in *engines* of the 'twenties has led to a current interest in *railways* all over the world. It has been well done.

A Wolverhampton King: No 6014 *King Henry VII* sits outside Stafford Road shed on a wet afternoon in November 1938

Castles and Saints: The semi-streamlined King No. 6019 *King Henry V* and Castle No 5005 *Manorbier Castle* stand in Swindon Works alongside No 2924 *Saint Helena* in 1937

Highland Railway: LMS 4-6-0 No 14766 *Clan Cameron* waits for her return train from Glasgow to Oban on the afternoon of September 16, 1937

Un-named 'Claughton': Ex-LNWR 4-6-0, then LMS No 5989 painted red and lined out in LMS colours at Crewe North Shed in the summer of 1933

Lancashire and Yorkshire Railway: Hughes superheated class B 4-6-0 at Manchester in April 1934

LMS-built to Derby design: 4-4-0 No 656 takes water outside the depot at Saltley, Birmingham in May 1936

LMS Sheds in Birmingham

Although England's second city could boast of first class train services to and from London its locomotive depots rarely, if ever, held any of the largest express engines. This was because the vast majority of trains ran straight through from Euston or Paddington to Wolverhampton, the capital of the Black Country conurbation, whose sheds at Bushbury and Stafford Road housed the Scots and the Kings. The LNW and later the LMS kept their leading express engines, Claughtons or Pacifics, to the main lines—Birmingham never saw them when they were new.

Right to the end of the steam era sheds were divided into three groups. Saltley and Bournville served the Midland division of the LMS, and Aston and Monument Lane the Western Division; Tyseley served the Great Western. The LMS Divisional Motive Power Superintendents were at Saltley and Bescot—the latter shed being part way between Birmingham and Wolverhampton, dealing solely with Western Division freight. The Great Western locomotive HQ was at Stafford Road, Wolverhampton. The Midland and Great Western sheds were roundhouses; the LNW preferred straight sheds.

During the 1930s Birmingham could boast a fair variety of locomotive classes, both pre-grouping and LMS Fowler and Stanier types. Jubilees were working the fastest Euston, Leeds and Bristol trains. Tyseley was still using Saints to work South Wales expresses via Stratford and Cheltenham. Aston would get ex-LNW Princes from Stafford and Manchester, and even the odd superheated Precursor from Rugby. Local services, semi-fast trains and freight workings provided a great deal of interest, for whilst the GWR had standardised its suburban trains with the 51xx tanks, some of the Stratford semi-fasts had Bulldogs, and in the early part of this period there were Counties on the South Wales trains via Stourbridge, Worcester and Hereford. The LMS was using its standard Fowler and Stanier 2-6-2 and 2-6-4 tanks on locals, but until the later 'thirties these were widely supplemented by ex-LNW engines on the Western division. For instance, as late as 1938 the fastest train of the evening to Sutton Coldfield was regularly hauled by a Webb 18in 0-6-2 tank.

Saltley Shed (i): Birmingham was the last home of the MR Kirtley double framed 0-6-0s. No 2812 is seen here at Saltley in the summer of 1931

Saltley Shed (ii): Ex-Midland Railway Class 3 4-4-0 No 771 was the pride of her crew in June 1935. These engines were, at that time, used mainly on the Birmingham–Worcester–Bristol semi-fasts

Bournville Shed (i): Ex-Midland 0-6-4 tank No 2033 stands stored during the summer of 1933. These engines, known locally as the 'hole in the wall tanks', were used on the New Street–Evesham–Ashchurch trains

Bournville Shed (ii): This depot was mainly a passenger one and was much smaller than the other Midland shed at Saltley. Here is unsuperheated ex-MR 4-4-0 No 369 in the late afternoon of September 3, 1938

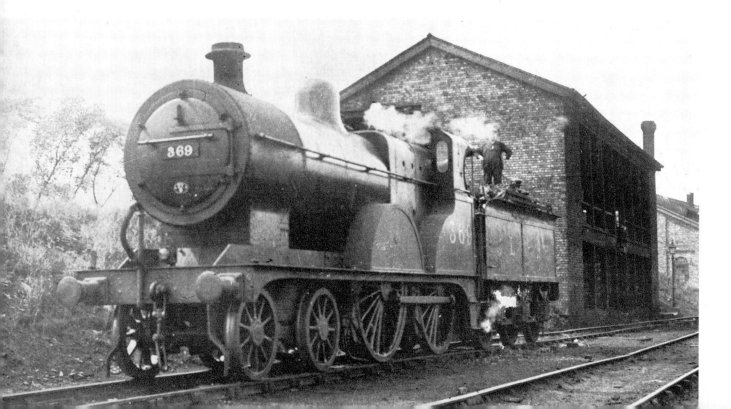

Bescot: This was an LNWR shed used entirely for freight working. Its main allocation for many years was the Super D Class 0-8-0. Here, in the early summer of 1946, some of these engines (nearly all fitted with Stanier chimneys) prepare for the day's work

Aston: This relatively small shed was to the LNW what Bournville was to the Midland. Its allocation consisted mostly of passenger engines—both main line and suburban. An evening in May of 1937 saw the then new 2-6-4 tank No 2611 waiting to go off shed to pick up a Coventry local

North Western Engines

Soon after Stanier took office at Crewe the slaughter of the pre-grouping engines absorbed into the LMS began in earnest, starting with the express classes. Like men of an older race hard pressed by an alien invader the Claughtons, Princes, Precursors and Jumbos retreated into the West and North. A few Claughtons went to the Midland division for a short while but most finished up working out their lives on the North Wales Coast based on Crewe, Chester and Llandudno Junction, as did a large number of the Princes, Georges and Precursors—the Jumbos were pressed even further North and West, to Cumberland on the one time Cockermouth, Keswick & Penrith line.

During this period I was part schoolboy, part student, and time and money were both somewhat limited—North Western engines therefore had to be sought at places not too far away. Naturally Crewe was a good place but the engines to be seen there were only too often waiting to be cut up—Stafford was a far better bet. Here there was a friendly shed master and friendly engine crews, which could lead to the coveted trip on the footplate of a semi-fast back home, and what a thrill that was. These trips usually took place after dark when Authority was safely out of the way—sixteen was a good age to learn to fire a loco and a rolling and rocking super-heated Precursor taught you to keep your feet, or else! But somehow the biggest thrill of all was getting a ride on the evening northbound train out of New Street. This was more often a Prince than a Precursor and although the load was not heavy, usually eight bogies, the sound and feel of her was something that I shall remember all my life. It wasn't just that—part of it was the anticipation—the train would come in from the Vauxhall carriage sidings down the bank into the South end tunnel, and to get her round the curve into the old No 3 platform the driver would open the regulator for a moment or two, put on the brakes gently and let her roll. As she came into sight there was that glorious LNW tink, tink, tink, which heralded the Georges and Princes and in the dark it was difficult at first to see just which class was coming—whether it was *Antaeus* or *Medusa* or *Queen of the Belgians*, or just plain 25752. But in the end no matter, for whatever the engine there was that climb up the bank through the big tunnel, past Monument Lane shed—first stop Dudley Port and on through all the Black Country lights. Goodbye was said at Wolverhampton, and I would return on the next fast, doing my best to remove the evidence in the toilet before going back on the bus to home and supper.

Lady of Crewe (i): After being taken out of service in the early 'thirties, the famous LNWR 2-4-0 *Hardwicke* was kept in Crewe paint shop for many years. Here she is in 1939 having been pulled out for photography. (The figure 1 of the ex-LMS number is still visible through the re-painting)

Lady of Crewe (ii): *Hardwicke's* splasher and nameplate

Engineer's Engine: After being used for a considerable time attached to the Crewe Engineer's Saloon, *Cornwall* was withdrawn early in the LMS period. She too was stored in the paint shop at Crewe until removal to Clapham museum

Cauliflower: These ubiquitous Webb engines lasted into the 1950s. Technically, they were classed as '18 inch goods' but they worked all types of traffic from trip freights to locals to the occasional fast excursion. No 8532 is seen here at Rugby in the autumn of 1934

Special Tank: Several of these ancient 0-6-0STs survived into the 1950s as works shunters at Crewe and Wolverton. This picture shows one of the latter engines in November 1958

Stafford Shed (i): In the 1930s the ex-LNWR Whale and Bowen Cooke 4-4-0s were still hard at work on express services. The original member of George Whale's fine Precursor class waits to go off shed to pick up a Rugby semi-fast in 1936

Stafford Shed (ii): the LNWR War Memorial *Patriot* in April 1934

Stafford Shed (v): The LNW Princes were regular inhabitants working trains to Rugby, Crewe via Stoke, or Shrewsbury. A latterday Prince No 25841 moves off the coaling stage in the summer of 1939

Stafford Shed (vi): No ex-LNWR mainline depot was often without a Super D. No 8078 stands ready for the road in the summer of 1939

Stafford Shed (iii): One of the superheated Precursors stabled at this depot for many years was No 25245 *Antaeus*. Here are details of her cabside and (iv) nameplate

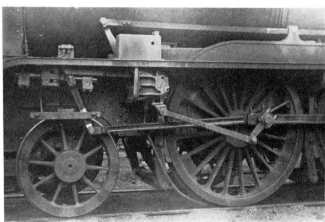

The Last Tishy: During LMS days a few of the LNWR Prince of Wales class 4-6-0s were rebuilt with a Walschaert's valve gear. No 25845 was actually built by the LMS with this gear and she lasted until 1947. For many years she was a Bletchley engine, as when these photographs were taken in 1946

The Last Queen: The last two named Princes were *Lusitania*, a Bletchley engine, and *Queen of the Belgians*, a Stafford engine. The latter is seen here on her home shed in June 1948

Coronation: No LNW series should be without this engine. She was the 5000th to be built at Crewe works and as one of the famous George V class she did magnificent work. She ended up at Stafford and was withdrawn in 1940

Sirocco: No 25297 finished her working life at Chester in 1949. She was the last LNWR 4-4-0 and would almost certainly have been preserved had she been able to continue into the more enlightened era that lay only a few years ahead. The photograph was taken at Chester in 1948

Coal Engines: These small LNW 0-6-0s were purely freight and shunting engines. Like some of the other small LNW classes, odd ones (as 58321 in 1948) ended up as works shunters and outlived their sisters

Some LNER Locos

The Grouping can almost be said to have consolidated a family of East Coast Railways, for the component lines of the LNER were already associated to a certain extent. In the south, the Great Central, Great Eastern and Great Northern were in alliance and the partnership of the latter with the North Eastern and North British was a long-standing one. Even the joining of the Group by the Great North of Scotland Railway seems quite natural when one considers this line's enmity with the Highland which became a part of the LMS.

All brought great locomotive traditions with them. The Great Northern with its apple green engines was the first to introduce the Atlantic type. The Great Central livery was a darker green; this company also possessed some magnificent machines, culminating in the Jersey Lily Atlantics, whilst the North Eastern's brass-capped, grass-green locomotives were a well-designed fleet with a strong family resemblance to each other. The Great Eastern used a distinctive ultramarine blue for its Claud Hamiltons and short-tendered 4-6-0s, and the North British with its bronze green locomotives produced the Scotts, the Glens and the fire-eating large-boilered Atlantics which looked so impressive in those F. Moore paintings and postcards. The other two lines—the Great North and the Hull and Barnsley painted their engines black, though the former had also used a green not unlike that of the Great Central.

The LNER carried on some of these separate traditions, though it was the first line in Britain to build Pacifics in large numbers, the only one to build 2-8-2s, and the first to introduce streamlining with the memorable A4s, one of which, *Mallard*, still holds the world's speed record for the steam locomotive.

That eminent historian and railwayman, George Dow, was an officer of the LNER and it has been partly through his writings, including the tremendous history of the Great Central, that we know these engines as well as we do. During the last years before nationalisation, Dow was the LNER Public Relations and Publicity Officer, and he made sure that not only were the company's feats publicised, but that no true enthusiast went without information properly requested. He was also responsible for seeing that those who sought them obtained the necessary permits for photography, hence LNER engines are particularly well recorded.

Thanks to Gresley's policy of using the best of the pre-grouping engines and maintaining them to a high standard, ex-LNER sheds produced a first class array of differing types and classes and these lasted well into the first decade of nationalisation. This meant that a visit to an Eastern or North Eastern Region shed was something to look forward to and it was in the North Eastern Region that the last and most modern steam depot of all, Thornaby, was completed as recently as the late 1950s.

Main Line Suburban (i): The LNER perpetuated the old Great Central Railway's 4-6-2T of 1911. These engines were used on the service out of Marylebone until the postwar years. No 5046 waits to take a northbound train out of London in May 1938

Main Line Suburban (ii): Inside cylinder tanks were also used for the old North British lines out of Glasgow and Edinburgh. Ex-NBR class C16 No 9515 stands on Eastfield shed in June 1939

GN Shed: Ivatt Atlantic then LNER No 3288 waits at
Kings Cross Shed in April 1937

NE Shed: LNER 4-4-2 No 2171 of class C9 (with
articulated bogie between loco and tender) sits on
Darlington Shed in August 1938. This engine fitted with
a booster, was rebuilt from an NER Class C7

NE 4-4-0: LNER Class D20 No 2023 at Middlesbrough
Shed in June 1938

GC 4-6-0: LNER Class B4 No 6102 in green livery arrives
at Scarborough Shed in July 1939

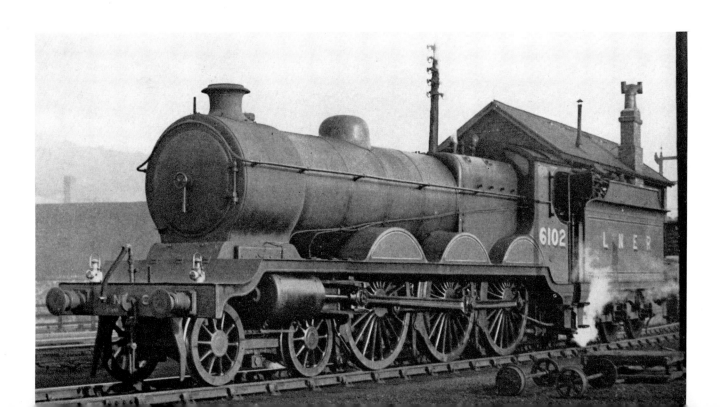

The Narrow Gauge in England

Somehow or other England never took to the narrow gauge—by the time that the mania for building these little railways was at its peak—1880–1900—almost everywhere that could have a railway in England had already got one. It was left to such remote places as Southwold, Waterhouses and Lynton to decide that the narrow road was the right one for them, but by the 1930s these good people had changed their minds. The Southwold was the first to go in 1929, the Leek and Manifold in 1934, and the Lynton and Barnstaple in 1935. Of these the Southwold and Lynton lines were seaside connections off the Great Main Line (and there was a time when it was possible to describe the East Suffolk line of the Great Eastern in just those terms). The Manifold line was more self important: it had engines based on those of the Barsi Light Railway in India, and it had transporter wagons to take standard gauge vehicles. If the Lynton and Southwold lines were pleasant and bucolic, the Manifold was Terrific and Unique. It also carried much less traffic, which no doubt gave it more time to take itself seriously. Still, it had the excuse of its surrounding scenery, which really was splendid.

There was one other English narrow gauge railway which should be mentioned—the Ashover. This was an offshoot of the Claycross Company in Derbyshire, serving quarries in the neighbourhood of Ashover and Fallgate. Like the Welsh Highland—a similar post-war product, it was of nominal 2ft 0in gauge and had as its engineer the redoubtable Col Stephens. Trains were powered by ex-WD Baldwin 4-6-0 tanks identical to the Welsh Highland's No 590. This was certainly the Indian Summer and the Ashover's timetable when it first opened was really like that of a town bus with two or three trains busily shuttling to and fro between the termini. Its headquarters and what passed for a works was at Ashover.

The two larger railways passed into the hands of the LMS and Southern Groups. The Manifold had its depot at Waterhouses where the two 2-6-4 tanks *E. R. Calthrop* and *J. B. Earle* lived in stately splendour and underwent normal maintainance and light repairs—the heavy work was carried out at Stoke in North Stafford days, and Crewe in the LMS period. The Lynton and Barnstaple had similar though larger facilities at Pilton, Barnstaple, and its engines in later years went to Eastleigh for heavy repairs. The Southwold railway stayed independent to the bitter end: from time to time it sent engines away for expert attention, but otherwise made do with spanners and sledgehammers.

In the 1920s and '30s there were also other interesting substandard gauge lines—miniature rather than narrow gauge. Of these probably the least known today is the Sand Hutton, and the best the Romney, Hythe and Dymchurch, plus of course tne now preserved Ravenglass and Eskdale. The latter was itself originally a true narrow gauge line closed in 1909 and resuscitated by a firm entitled Narrow Gauge Railways Ltd. which was connected with the well-known model making Company, Bassett-Lowke. The conversion to 15in gauge was completed during the first world war, in 1917. The locomotive shed was then, and still is, at Ravenglass.

Leek & Manifold (i): 2-6-4T *E. R. Calthrop* at Waterhouses

Leek & Manifold (ii): General view of loco shed at Waterhouses in 1930. Loco on left is *E. R. Calthrop* and on right, *J. B. Earle.* These were the first 2-6-4 tanks to run in Britain

Lynton & Barnstaple Railway: 2-6-2T then Southern
Railway No 759 *Yeo* at Barnstaple in August 1934

Southwold Railway:
2-4-0T No 2 *Halesworth*
at Southwold in August
1923

Sand Hutton Light Railway: Hunslet-built No 12 *Esme*
at Bossall in May 1927

Ravenglass and Eskdale
Railway: 15in gauge
4-6-2 at Ravenglass in
1925

The Narrow Gauge in Wales and the Isle of Man

In the 1920s the Isle of Man Railway was a busy line with what would today be considered considerable traffic, but it faced difficult times for in the latter half of the decade newly-incorporated bus undertakings were providing fierce competition. By the time the photographs reproduced here were taken by Alfred Croughton relief had come: the Railway Company had bought out its two rival road undertakings and felt it had thereby purchased prosperity. At that time the IoMR owned sixteen engines, all but one being 2-4-0 tanks and all built between 1873 and 1926 by Beyer, Peacock of Manchester. No locomotives were built between 1910 and 1926 when the final engine No 16 *Mannin* appeared; this locomotive was larger and more powerful than her sisters and was put into traffic on the more heavily-graded and popular Port Erin line. Most were shedded at Douglas but there were also small single road sheds at Peel, Port Erin and Ramsey. Isle of Man Railway livery at this period was bright green with a black band having a fine vermilion line each side.

In Wales the Indian Summer of the narrow gauge was drawing towards its close and the following photographs show locomotives of three lines, each of which was quite different in character. The first, the 2ft 4½in gauge Glyn Valley Tramway, was based on Chirk almost on the English border. It was primarily a line serving quarries along the valley of the River Ceiriog, but it also carried passengers. Being a roadside tramway it succumbed early—in 1935—its Beyer, Peacock tram engines and the sole American ex-WD Baldwin being broken up at Chirk by the end of the summer. Fortunately one of the nameplates from the tram engine *Glyn* came into the author's hands via Messrs Davies of Barmouth and this is now on loan to the Narrow Gauge Museum at Towyn.

Next comes the Talyllyn, a 2ft 3in gauge line based on Towyn in Merioneth and running in an easterly direction for some seven miles to the small village of Abergynolwyn which is almost nowhere. This now famous line, the first ever to be preserved by a group of enthusiasts, was a slate railway, opened in 1865, which also carried passengers from the outset. By the late 1930s slate was still quarried but the line was very run down. It still had all its original track and equipment, and its two locomotives, *Talyllyn* and *Dolgoch*, had had very little attention.

Lastly the Newest and Whitest Elephant of them all, the Welsh Highland. Taking over and extending the bankrupt and moribund North Wales Narrow Gauge Railway, it was opened to traffic in stages in 1922/3, and acquired a motley collection of locomotives, having no money to purchase anything designed specially. Trains ran on the 1ft 11½in line only until 1937—the line was too long and built too late.

Isle of Man (i): Beyer, Peacock-built 2-4-0T No 2 *Derby* at Douglas in 1926

Isle of Man (ii): New and enlarged 2-4-0T No 16 *Mannin* at Douglas in 1926

Talyllyn Railway: 0-4-2ST No 1 *Talyllyn* and 0-4-0T No 2 *Dolgoch* at Towyn Pendre in September 1939

Glyn Valley Tramway: 0-4-2T No 3 *Glyn* at Chirk in June 1925

Welsh Highland Railway (i): 0-6-4T *Moel Tryfan*: 1925

Welsh Highland Railway (ii): Scene at Dinas Junction in 1925 depicting 4-6-0T No 590

The Narrow Gauge in Ireland

In 1924 Alfred Croughton took his camera to Ireland and 'did the sheds' on the narrow gauge. Posterity must be eternally grateful to him for his records are comprehensive and extremely valuable—few exist in so thorough a form and Irish narrow gauge photographs before this date are comparatively rare. THE year to go was 1924 and Croughton with his heavy quarter plate camera, complete with glass negatives, made a job of it—turning doubtful hotel bedrooms into dark-rooms and humping great cases full of delicate and heavy plates from town to town and village to village. It was all done by train in the last year of the various lines' independence, for in 1925 there came the great Irish amalgamation—everything not crossing the Border went into the bag and came out as the Great Southern.

So in the following pages can be found pictures of ancient and intriguing narrow gauge engines sitting outside their sheds during the late evening of their independence. Croughton was a collector of locomotive records, for in those days it was difficult enough to take pictures of many trains on the main line—one needed a pantechnicon full of gear—cameras with swing front and swing back, plates, tripod and patience. This was fair enough when trains came past every hour or so, but on the narrow gauge not so easy. Usually there were but two or three trains each way per day so that once you had taken your lineside picture there was nothing more to photograph for most of the day. The only answer was shed shots and engine portraits and we must be thankful to have these.

The Irish narrow gauge was standardised—all lines were 3ft 0in gauge—some were built as tramways but most were Light Railways. Most had their own repair shops at the principal depot and many of these were capable of carrying out all but the heaviest repairs. On the formation of the Great Southern most of these shops were run down or closed, the heavy repair jobs going to Inchicore, Dublin.

But even in GSR days the men were independent even if their lines were not, and there is the tale of the private strike they had one time at Ballinamore, the headquarters of the Cavan and Leitrim section. Mr. H——— from Dublin went down to settle it. Johnny G——— was the men's spokesman and as he was showing him into where the Great Man was, the foreman tells him to take off his hat. No damn fear of course; in walks Johnny (a fine big man) and his hat on the back of his head.

'Do you know who I am?' said Mr. H in his gruff voice.

'No,' says Johnny, and he knowing full well.

'I am Mr. H,———the Running Superintendent of the Great Southern Railway.'

'And I,' says Johnny 'Am Driver Johnny G——— of the Cavan and Leitrim Railway.' Whereupon the meeting broke up in disorder.

Schull and Skibbereen Railway: One of the original 0-4-0 tanks, No 2 *Ida,* at Skibbereen in May 1924

Tralee & Dingle Light Railway: 2-6-0 No 1 in old company livery at Tralee in May 1924

Cork & Muskerry Light Railway (i): 0-4-4 tank No 6
Muskerry at Cork (Western Road) in May 1924

Cork & Muskerry Light Railway (ii): 4-4-0 tank No 4
Blarney also at Cork (Western Road) in May 1924

Cork, Blackrock & Passage Railway: 2-4-2 tank No 7
at Passage in May 1924

Cavan & Leitrim Railway: 4-4-0 tank No 3—*Lady Edith*
(now preserved in USA) at Ballinamore in May 1924

County Donegal: 4-6-2T *Mourne* stands outside the shed at Stranorlar, the locomotive headquarters of the line in 1933

LMS (NCC): 4-4-2T of class T, once belonging to the Ballycastle Railway, stands at Larne in July, 1937

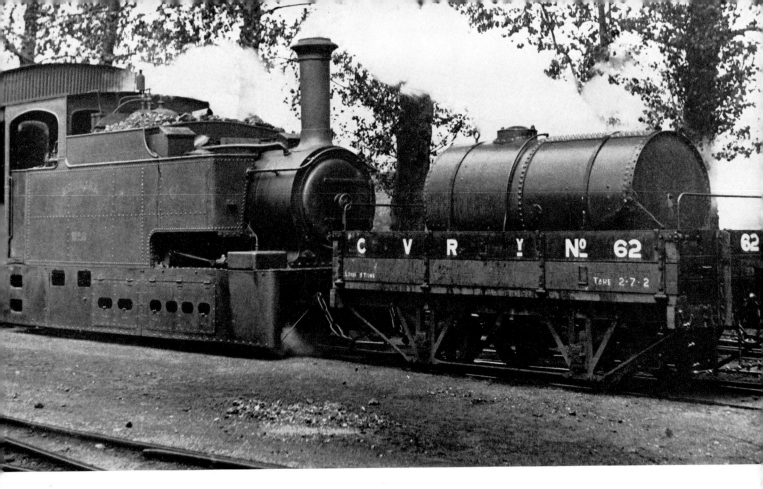

Clogher Valley (i):
No 2 *Errigal,* a
Sharp Stewart
0-4-2T, with weed
killer wagon at
Aughnacloy in July,
1933

Clogher Valley (ii):
Scene on the shed
at Aughnacloy in
July, 1933

Londonderry and Lough Swilly (i) : Scene on the shed at Derry in September, 1937

Londonderry and Lough Swilly (ii) : Scene on the shed at Letterkenny in May, 1934

Monorail, Listowel and Ballybunnion: No 1 waits out of service at Listowel in 1924

Giant's Causeway tram: No 3 *Dunluce Castle*, a Wilkinson 0-4-0 tram engine, waits
outside its shed in July, 1933

Postwar—The LMS Scene

The early years of nationalisation were the beginning of the new era in railway photography—better cameras were starting to be available and films were becoming faster with less grain. Time, however, was running out fast—the scrapping programme, halted during the war years, was once more in full swing; and new standard classes of locomotive, although still of company design, were beginning to replace the old pre-grouping warriors which had been temporarily spared the torch.

Nowhere was this more apparent than on the LMS lines. True, Stanier had made great inroads into the older engines in the 1930s but there was still plenty to be seen, and in addition there were one's favourite express engines to be recorded either in the old LMS livery or in one of the new and ever changing British Railways' styles. There was a feeling of urgency in the air, for new 'standard' locomotives were on the drawing boards, branches were closing and there was talk of diesels for the future.

The ex-LMS sheds, grimy and dirty though they were, provided more variety than any other Region. Some, like Camden and Speke and Stafford, were comparatively new; most of the larger depots had huge reinforced concrete coaling plants; but otherwise they dated back unchanged to the days of the LMS's predecessors—the Old Companies. Here, even in the London area you could find Bowen Cooke Super Ds alongside Stanier 8Fs and even at Camden there were still some ancient long chimney Webb Coal engines used as carriage pilots and bankers at Euston. At Crewe, Compounds and Duchesses sat end to end waiting for coal, water, or disposal whilst at Carlisle Caley 4-4-0s rubbed shoulders with Scots, Black 5s and Crabs.

Further from the main line—on detachment as it were—one would find the elder brethren. Almost forgotten classes like ex-Furness 0-6-0s at Moor Row, LNW Cauliflower 0-6-0s at Penrith, Webb 2-4-2 tanks at Warwick, Milverton and ancient Midland 2-4-0s at Gloucester. If you looked hard enough you could find even more unusual oddments still at work. For instance the Cromford and High Peak section housed a sole LNWR survivor—2-4-0T No 26428—in the tiny shed at Sheep Pasture. Bournville had some double framed Kirtley 0-6-0s for use on the Halesowen branch and Chester had 25297 *Sirocco*, the last LNWR superheated Precursor which was also the last LNWR express passenger engine. She was nearly kept for posterity and sat at Crewe in hope for several months after withdrawal but it was not to be. A great and cardinal error.

Early Jubilee: No 45571 *South Africa,* one of the first of her class, sits outside Camden shed in June 1962

Camden Pacific: With a 'not to be moved' sign sticking out of her tender, a de-streamlined Duchess stands outside the shed in June 1952. She is No 46239 City of Chester

Royal Scot: A portrait of No 46118 *Royal Welch Fusilier* at Camden in August 1951

Furness Engine: Moor Row shed in Cumberland still had three of these 0-6-0s in 1950. No 52494 was the only survivor to carry her Furness boiler, the other two having L & Y boilers

Big Bertha: The Lickey banker, still with 'LMS' on her tender but re-numbered 58100, waits for a train at Bromsgrove in August, 1949

Old and New: An ex-LNWR Super D 0-8-0 meets one of her successors in an LMS 8F 2-8-0 at Carlisle in September 1954

Postwar—The Southern Scene

Although the Southern Railway was the smallest of the 'Big Four' its prewar locomotive policy (or rather, lack of one) provided the enthusiasts with a large number of locomotive classes some of which were of considerable vintage. The early years of nationalisation appeared to make little difference to the policy in spite of the advent of the Bulleid Pacifics for heavy and intermediate express work. In particular the Kent Coast and South Western depots housed pre-grouping designs of 4-4-os which outlived their sisters from other railways by several years.

On the Kent coast lines one found enough variety on summer weekends to satisfy the most fastidious enthusiast. A visit to Ramsgate over Whitsun in 1958 produced Bulleid light pacifics, King Arthur 4-6-os, Schools 4-4-0, and at least two classes of Moguls. In addition there were ex-SE&CR 4-4-os of four types: the German-built pre-first World War L class, their Maunsell improvements the L.1s, and two Wainwright classes, the D.1s and E.1s plus some 0-4-4s and odd 0-6-os.

If one went to Brighton at the same time there would have been almost as many classes but most of these would be quite different. A common denominator would be the King Arthurs but there were also considerable numbers of ex-LB&SC engines including the last Atlantics to run in Great Britain—Marsh's *Beachy Head* and *South Foreland*. More mundane locos were LB&SC Moguls, 0-6-os and 0-6-2 tanks all in exceptionally clean condition, for the Southern too was showing considerable pride in the external condition of its engines in 1957/8. Brighton had three other engines of note at that time, for the restored Terrier *Boxhill* and the LSWR Adams 4-4-0 were kept there waiting to go to the new BR Museum at Clapham. Last but far from least was the Brighton Works Terrier proudly repainted in her old LBSC 'improved engine green'—and she was at work every day as smart as a new pin.

The South Western Section was pretty good too. On the whole its engines apart from the Big Bulleids were not so clean but there was plenty to see. Sheds like Exmouth Junction would have all classes of Pacifics, LSW H.15 4-6-os, two classes of Maunsell Moguls, two classes of LSW 0-4-4 tanks (M7 and O2), ex-LMS 1200 Class 2-6-2 tanks, and the odd LSW T.9 or 0-6-0. But it was to the very South and West that the faithful went since at Wadebridge there were three ancient old ladies; the Beattie 2-4-0 well tanks specially kept for the Wenford Bridge mineral trains and for working the harbour.

Yes, the Southern in those days was worth seeing.

Ramsgate (i): Until the South Eastern Electrification the Kent coast lines had a great variety of motive power. In 1957 Ramsgate offered, among others, West Countrys, King Arthurs, Schools, Moguls, and ex-SE&CR 0-6-0s

Ramsgate (ii): In 1957 the Ramsgate washout engine was this unknown SE&CR D class 4-4-0

Ramsgate (iii): A BR standard class 5 and Battle of Britain and West Country Pacifics Nos 34088 *213 Squadron* and 34017 *Ilfracombe* in June 1957

Ramsgate (iv): Schools class No 30935 *Sevenoaks* in June 1957

Beattie Tank (i): One of the three Wadebridge sisters, No 30587, in August 1956. These engines were used on the Wenford Bridge mineral line

Beattie Tank (ii): Close up
of crosshead and springing
arrangement for 30587 at
Wadebridge in 1956

Brighton Atlantic: the last Atlantics to run in Great Britain were those built by the LBSCR. Here is No 32421 *South Foreland* at Portsmouth in July 1953

Ashford 4-4-0: German-built L class No 31777 sits on the turntable at Ashford in August, 1957

Reading (i): Full face portrait of ex-SE&CR D class 4-4-0 No 31496 in May 1953

Reading (ii): N class Moguls 31827 and 31865 with D class No 31075 sandwiched between in June 1954

Brighton Mogul: LB&SCR 2-6-0 No 32347 on the shed at Brighton in April 1957

Postwar—The Great Western Scene

When nationalisation came to British railways on January 1, 1948 the companies making up the Big Four were dissolved. In their place there sprang up five Regions and the Great Western Railway. Whether this was right or wrong is a matter of opinion, but without doubt during the pre-Raymond period at Paddington the pride and spirit of the Great Western was still there and apparent to its passengers. This pride was equally obvious to the railway enthusiast who was able to see the gradual but steady improvement in the condition of the Western Region locomotives from their dirty unkempt wartime appearance to the new green paint so carefully applied at Swindon towards the end of the 1950s.

There were certain sheds, some small and some large, which did better than others in this respect. Old Oak vied with Stafford Road, Wolverhampton for the smartness of its Kings; Bristol, Bath Road had splendid Castles which carried the names of their drivers for the new 'Bristolian' and Danny Rowlands at Aberystwyth kept his Manors for the 'Cambrian' superbly. Cardiff Canton became known for its carefully turned out engines, and deserves an especially good mark for being willing to modify its GWR loyalties sufficiently to get good work out of the Britannias, which almost only here on the Western repeated the sound performances they achieved elsewhere. Even the pilots provided by Newton Abbot for the drags over Dainton and Rattery gleamed in the Devon sunshine. These were happy days for the railway photographer, for clean engines made good pictures.

But perhaps the *pièce de resistance* was an inhabitant of a relatively small Berkshire shed—Didcot. In 1957 Reggie Hanks, then Chairman of the Western Region Board, arranged with the agreement of the Curator of Historical Relics to take the famous *City of Truro* out of York Museum and put her back into service for use on special excursions. She was duly put through Swindon Works and reappeared resplendent for duty. Her home was Didcot where she was used regularly on the light Newbury and Southampton turns to make her earn her daily bread in addition to the jam.

So it was that whilst the Western Region did not have the variety of the London Midland or Eastern sheds it did provide its own particular interest —a last Indian summer of smart engines looked after by men who cared for them in the old tradition.

Bristol (i): Saint class 4-6-0 No 2981 *Ivanhoe* stands at St Philips Marsh in a somewhat dirty condition. The date is October 1948

Bristol (ii): Another Saint—this time No 2954, comes off Bath Road shed on the same date. She was one of the later Saints and was named *Tockenham Court*

Bristol (iii): Looking across from the down platform at Temple Meads station one could easily see the locomotives coming on and off Bath Road shed. Here is No 7036 *Taunton Castle* leaving the depot to head the up 'Merchant Venturer'

Tyseley: Still with the wartime cover over the ashpit road. Saint class No 2950 *Taplow Court* awaits her day's duty in October 1950

Bulldog nameplate: *Vancouver*—No 3401—was one of the few of her class to survive the war; this picture was taken in 1947

Aberystwyth: The regular engine for the 'Cambrian Coast Express' for the summer of 1964

Unlikely Bedfellows: During the war the GWR took over the late Weston, Clevedon & Portishead Light Railway. Here is one of that line's Terrier Tanks at Bristol St Philips Marsh shed in 1946

The Great King: Still at work on the London expresses in 1961, *King George V* stands ready for the road at Wolverhampton Stafford Road shed

Wenlock Engine: Small wheeled 2-6-2 tank No 4409 (used on the Wellington—Much Wenlock—Craven Arms service) stands outside Stafford Road Works, Wolverhampton, in October 1949

Castles at Stafford Road: No 4076 *Carmarthen
Castle* and 7008 *Swansea Castle* at the coaling
stage in September 1957 and February 1958
respectively

LNER and LMS in Scotland

The great thing about Scotland from the railway photographer's point of view was that you could almost always make your shot into a *picture* as well as a record. Not that this really applied everywhere with shed shots: but it wasn't too inaccurate particularly once you got off the beaten track. For instance the backdrops to Fort William and Mallaig sheds were Ben Nevis and the Island of Skye respectively whilst Oban and Lossiemouth not only had magnificent engines but superb sea views if only the sun shone.

But whatever the weather the sheds in the Highlands had something: even places where locos had been standardised for years often produced an odd interloper. For example the Highland Line was awash with Black Fives, but it had a sprinkling of Caley Bogies on pilot duties out of Blair Atholl and Aviemore or on the occasional local: while Caley 0-4-4 tanks pounded up and down the Killin or Ballachulish branches, or shunted cattle trucks at Kyle of Lochalsh. Sheds on the Great North of Scotland had ancient warriors like the now preserved *Gordon Highlander*, and even a set of Great Eastern design B12 class 4-6-0s. Thurso housed the last two Bens (*Alder* and *Vrackie*) and Dornoch, a Highland 0-4-4 tank later replaced by, of all things, a Swindon-built 16xx class 0-6-0 pannier tank. And last but far from least the West Highland still saw K2s, K4s, and Glens.

One of the odder things the LNER locomotive department did was to make a practice of doubleheading West Highland trains with ex-GNR K2 2-6-0s and ex-NBR Glen 4-4-0s: a rare combination, but marvellous to listen to, with three- and two-cylinder exhausts combining. For years these engines worked the Glasgow—Fort William trains in tandem and this just lasted into the 1950s. To go to Fort William and stand in the shadow of Ben Nevis on a spring evening was something to remember in any event but in the early 1950s you could look across at the shed and go back twenty years—there were times when there was not a post-grouping engine in sight. But somehow it was the Glens which made it and in May 1958 two of them, *Glen Falloch* and *Glen Loy* backed down from the shed to the station to take for the last time a regular scheduled train home to Glasgow in tandem.

'Toram Beg', Norman McKillop the well-known ex-NB driver and journalist tells a story of the Glens. One day before the last war he stopped at Thornton with the then new Gresley *Cock o' the North*—the biggest engine with the biggest train ever to run the road. It was over 600 tons on the test run—about twice the capacity of a Glen. During the few minutes they stood at the station a local driver from Thornton Junction Shed gave the brand new *Cock* a look over. After he had satisfied his curiosity McKillop asked him if he liked her.

'Ach, no' said Sandy, 'Ye'd be better wi' a guid Glen!'

Fort William Shed (i): The early 1950s still produced an almost prewar atmosphere on the West Highland. Fort William shed in the autumn of 1953 housed at least one Glen (Glen Mamie) as well as named K2s, K1s and ex-North British 0-6-0s

Fort William Shed (ii): May 1958 saw the special working of two Glen class 4-4-0s on regular trains to Fort William for television purposes. Nos 62496 *Glen Loy* and 62471 *Glen Falloch*. Here is *Glen Loy* on the shed

Great Eastern Wanderer: The ex-GER B12 class 4-6-0 proved very popular on the old Great North of Scotland lines of the LNER and later Scottish Region. A clean member of the class, No 61560, stands at Elgin in August 1950

Scottish Director: The LNER built some additions to the Great Central Director class 4-4-0s. Here is No 62671 *Bailie Mac-Wheeble* at Inverurie in August 1953

Great North 4-4-0: D41 class ex-GNSR No 62228 waits to go off shed at Elgin in August 1950

Small Ben: Still carrying her LMS number and livery, No 14410 *Ben Dearg* comes on to the shed at Forres in October 1950

Highland Shed: The depot yard at Inverness, taken from the shed roof in October 1951

Highland Works: Clan Goods class No 57954 under repair in Lochgorm Works, Inverness, in October 1950

Some Smaller Engines

By the early 1950s most of the larger pre-grouping engines had gone and their smaller brethren were beginning to be replaced by more modern motive power. But there was still plenty to see if you looked hard enough, Midland 0-4-4 tanks at Evercreech Junction on the Somerset & Dorset, Great Eastern station pilots at Liverpool Street, Caley 0-4-4 tanks at Oban or Killin and North British 4-4-2 tanks at Craigendoran. On the whole the tank engines lasted longer than tender engines especially on passenger work but even so the latter too could be seen at work at various outposts of the BR Empire. For instance LMS 4-4-0s of Class 2 were hard at it on pilot work on the S&D. LSWR T.9 4-4-0s rambled round the North Devon and Cornwall lines, Glens and Scotts did sterling duty in Scotland and the Great Western Dukedogs were regular engines on the Cambrian Coast—even to heading that famous but short-lived named train from time to time. Most of the Dukedogs gravitated to the Cambrian section, being based on Machynlleth and its various sub sheds. Mostly they did passenger work but every now and again one turned up with the daily goods.

Machynlleth was always a good shed to visit as it was easily accessible and housed not only the Dukedogs but other delightful engines such as Cambrian 0-6-0s (Nos 884, 873, 892, 894 and 896 among others), Manors and the small wheeled GWR 45xx and 55xx 2-6-2 tanks—these in particular were excellent engines for the coast line. A summer Saturday would strain Machynlleth to its utmost for in addition to having to provide coast line engines it had to cope with the Talerddig bankers as well—and at that time practically all Saturday trains were loaded to over seven coaches and therefore needed assistance on the 1 in 54.

The other shed with which I always connect pilots and bankers was Bath (Green Park) on the Somerset & Dorset. Again it was summer Saturdays which taxed it to a high degree for the 4-6-0s and light Pacifics used as train engines could rarely cope with the heavy through trains from the North. It is sad that this traffic is now gone and the line taken up, and one wonders whether the passenger has gained by the re-routing. From 1949 to 1951 my wife and I went regularly to Ossie Nock's famous summer holiday weekends on the S&D. Looking back now the whole scene is almost unbelievable—between 10am and 6pm trains were pounding up the banks to and from Bath, engines labouring up the twisting gradients and running as fast as they dared down the other side. All types and classes they were—ex-MR and LMS 4-4-0s in the main acting as pilots. Literally everything Bath shed had in working order was pressed into service—there were even occasions when the Radstock shunter, a 'Jinty' 0-6-0 tank was used as a pilot running bunker first and the following train was headed by a pair of S&D 2-8-0s.

Bath S&D: Green Park shed rarely saw Moguls but in August 1951 this Stanier 2-6-0 No 42963 made an appearance

Galashiels: The Fife trains until the mid 1950s were often headed by Scots or Glens of the old NBR. No 62484 *Glen Lyon* came from Thornton in August 1953

Warwick, Milverton: This depot sheltered the engines for the branch line services to Rugby and Weedon. In 1949 the LNWR tanks for push and pull services were superseded by the newer ex-LMS 1200s. In this case 46749 and 41228

GE Survivor: Stratford shed provided J69 class 0-6-0T No 68619 in October 1959. She was used as Liverpool Street Station pilot and painted in Great Eastern Railway colours

Worcester 0-4-2T: No 3574 was, in June 1948, the last survivor of the open cab ex-GWR 0-4-2 tanks

Machynlleth (i): Dukedog No 9001 with thin chimney in August 1953 when these engines were still working regularly on the Cambrian Coast

Machynlleth (ii): Collett 0-6-0 No 3202 on the table in June 1955

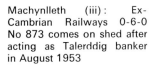

Machynlleth (iii): Ex-Cambrian Railways 0-6-0 No 873 comes on shed after acting as Talerddig banker in August 1953

Smaller Tank Engines

During the decade that followed World War II it was still possible to visit dozens of country sheds, spread pretty widely over the face of Britain, and find that they were the home of some small veteran of pre-grouping days. Apart from the well-known survivors like the Beattie tanks at Wadebridge or the Highland 0-4-4s at Dornoch one could find many others, a little more mundane perhaps but still old engines in the evening of their days.

The Isle of Wight lines were then still resisting the Southern Region's attempts to kill them off, and the little O.2 class 0-4-4 tanks emerged daily from Newport or Ryde St John's in green complete with brass nameplates duly polished. Other limbs of the Southern still heard the chaff-chaff of the Westinghouse pump from the O.2s larger sisters, the LSW M.7s; these could be found over most of the Western section of the Region from Seaton to Southampton and from Lymington even to the portals of Waterloo where they acted as station pilots and carriage shunters until the early 1960s.

The Western had fewer tank engines of such great age as the GW standardised its classes early and had replaced nearly all its light-duty fleet by the 1930s. By far the most ubiquitous were the 57xx class 0-6-0 pannier tanks: even today some of them are still at work for London Transport, running engineers' trains from Neasden depot, replacing the old Metropolitan 0-4-4 and 0-6-2 tanks. The smaller ex-GW sheds were also likely to contain either a 14xx class Collett 0-4-2 tank or possibly a 64xx 0-6-0 pannier tank built for passenger rather than shunting work. Examples of the former could be found at places as far away as Abingdon or Penmaenpool—the 0-6-0 tanks taking the more hilly terrain in South Wales, the Black Country or such lines as the Bala–Blaenau Festiniog branch. There were also some BR-built, Swindon-designed small wheeled 0-6-0 tanks. These were the 16xx series, constructed to replace the older 2021 Class, and allocated to more lightly laid branches. They could be found in abundance at Lydney shed on the erstwhile Severn & Wye, and one even got as far north as the Dornoch branch in its later years, replacing the old Highlanders. Fortunately examples of these GWR engines can still be seen at work based on Buckfastleigh in Devon. They now belong to the privately owned Dart Valley Light Railway.

The LMS had great variety, and its successor the LMR did not dispose of all its relics for some years. On the whole they kept to their native territory and some very odd survivors remained in corners of the works at Crewe and Wolverton—North Western engines could also be found at branch sheds like Newport Pagnell and Aylesbury (0-6-2 coal tank) or Walsall (Webb 2-4-2 tank). The Midland Railway was represented by its 0-4-4 tanks at such sheds as Wirksworth, or Highbridge on the S&D, whilst the L&Y 2-4-2 tanks were hard at work from Newton Heath, Manchester. In Scotland it was the Caledonian 0-4-4 tanks which were to the fore and not only were they to be seen in the mountains round Killin or Ballachulish but they also sometimes turned up at Glasgow Central.

Engines from the LNER were spread further afield—there were even some old Great Northern 4-4-2 tanks still at work. These could be seen at Dukeries Junction or on the Seaton–Stamford line near Peterborough: some stayed on their original London suburban duties until the Alexandra Palace branch closed in the mid-fifties. Until then, Great Central 4-4-2 tanks worked out of Gorton, Manchester on the CLC and North British engines of the same wheel arrangement could be seen at Edinburgh. The NB engines were well sought after in their later years; the last of all were shedded at Arrochar and Tarbet to work the West Highland service to Craigendoran. Then there were the North Eastern 0-4-4 tanks and their Great Eastern 0-4-4 and 2-4-2 sisters, plus the oddest of them all—the 0-6-0 tram engine on the Wisbech & Upwell tramway. It certainly was an interesting decade.

Loco Condemned (i) : Former Rhymney Railway 0-6-2 tank, later GWR and BR No 33, awaits her fate at Swindon

Loco Condemned (ii) : The last of the GWR saddle tanks, No 1925, in the dump at Swindon in 1950

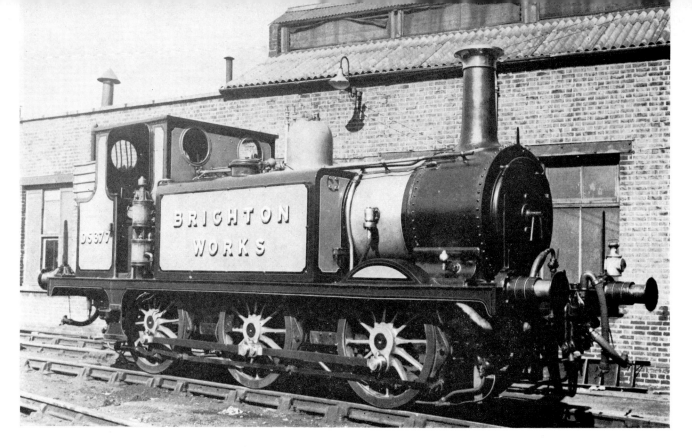

Brighton Works: During the later '50s, when the Regions were given more autonomy, several of them used this opportunity to paint engines in prewar or pre-grouping liveries. The Southern was no exception and this works Terrier at Brighton was seen in Stroudley's 'improved engine green' in April 1957

Brighton Shed: On the same Sunday the shed at Brighton was full of pre-grouping engines including ex-LB&SCR 0-6-2 tank No 32508

Crewe Shunter: Several ancient tank engines survived far longer than their normal span as works shunters. This ex-LNWR 'Bissell Truck' 0-4-2 tank was still at work at Crewe in 1949

Oxford Shed: This was one of the last depots open for steam in the Western Region. Oxford housed a variety of classes and right to the end one of the small Collett 0-4-2 tanks could be found there. No 1442 is now preserved and stands on a plinth at Tiverton, Devon. She was photographed here in May 1960

Neasden Shed: This picture of L48 was taken in May 1963; the LT engines did not survive long after that. They were replaced by ex-WR 57xx class pannier tanks. Some of these are still at work in 1969

LMS Giant: Probably the finest engine to be built by any British railway was the Stanier Pacific. Here is one of the last and greatest of them all—No 46256 *Sir William A. Stanier F.R.S.*—at Crewe in August 1963

Pick of

LNER Giant: Gresley A4 Pacifics will be close contenders for the title of the finest class and well they deserve this honour too. One of the early engines, No 60014 *Silver Link*, is seen here at Kings Cross shed in July 1952

Swindon Racer: the GWR Castles and their BR-built sisters were superb steam engines and at one time or another were on all the principal Western expresses. One of the 1950-built engines complete with double chimney waits at Bath Road Depot, Bristol, in May 1964

Bunch

Southern Hero: The Lord Nelsons were the Southern's largest engines, but they never really achieved the fame or following of the Duchesses, A4s or Castles. During the last part of its life No 30851 *Sir Francis Drake* found itself at Eastleigh in January 1956

Ireland, North and South

Northern Ireland (Belfast, York Road Shed) is now the last bastion of regular steam working in Great Britain, but the Republic of Ireland was in fact the first of the countries concerned to be wholly dieselised. It is now twenty years since nationalisation came to Northern Ireland and twenty one since the 1947 fuel famine which caused havoc (and turf burning, which amounted to the same thing) in the South; both these events were the forerunners of the closure of Ireland's steam sheds.

The picture in 1947 was very similar to that existing before the War. A visit then to either North or South would have provided a variety of locomotive types and classes that had to be seen to be believed: for few of the Irish lines ever built many engines of one class and there were red engines, blue engines, green engines and black engines ranging from 4-6-os to 2-4-os and from large Baltic tanks to 2-4-2Ts. Ireland was a country of 4-4-os—admittedly the CIE (ex-Great Southern) had a small number of 4-6-os and a few Moguls made from parts supplied by Woolwich and Ashford after World War I, but most of the passenger engines were 4-4-os and what a magnificent lot they were.

Without any doubt at all the prize went to the Great Northern of Ireland which had at least four classes of 4-4-0 arrayed in sky blue and scarlet, and even its black engines were kept spotless. A visit to Adelaide shed at Belfast to see these machines even in their later years, was always a day to be remembered. Other centres of importance where this type predominated were York Road Shed at Belfast with its red Derby-built engines (some named after castles), and Inchicore, the Great Southern's Dublin shed and works. Here one would see glossy black engines from the old Great Southern & Western, which somehow showed their relationship with Crewe via McConnell; and other massive inside-cylinder locomotives from the old Midland Great Western.

Back at Belfast there was the Queen's Quay shed of the Belfast & County Down, a line which mainly used tank engines. This railway ran a concentrated suburban service out to Bangor (Co. Down) and frequent trains to Donaghadee and Newcastle. Most of them were hauled by Beyer, Peacock-built 4-4-2Ts but the Bangor trains were also headed by Ireland's only Baltics. It was the County Down which got the axe first and now only the Bangor line remains—populated by diesel multiple units. The old shed was used for some ten years afterwards to store withdrawn locomotives for sale to scrap dealers and it was a melancholy sight to see them there in the late 'fifties and early 'sixties marked in chalk with lot numbers.

Now there are only the 'Jeeps' (Derby-built 2-6-4 tanks) working the muck trains in and out of Belfast to help motorway construction, and these will not last much longer.

Sky Blue & Scarlet (i): S Class 4-4-0 No 170 *Errigal* in Great Northern blue stands on Adelaide shed, Belfast, in April 1960

Sky Blue & Scarlet (ii): 4-4-0 No 58 *Lagan* waits for a Dublin excursion on Adelaide shed, Belfast, in April 1960

Great Northern 0-6-0 : Ulster Transport
Authority No 47 waits to go off shed at
Belfast, Adelaide in April 1960. She
was used to work a local to Portadown

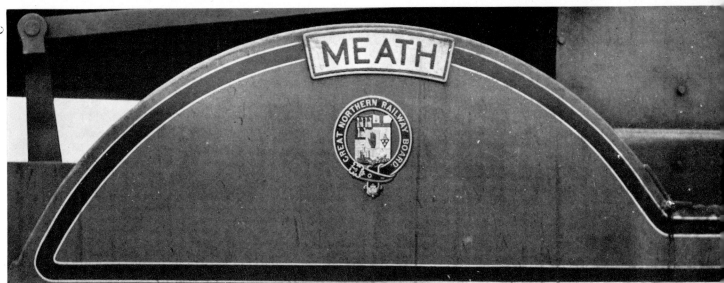

Small 4-4-0 (i): Ex-Great Northern of Ireland 4-4-0 No 201 *Meath* on the turntable at Bundoran in August 1958. She had worked the 'Bundoran Express' from Dublin

Small 4-4-0 (ii): Close up of name-plate and Great Northern Railway Board crest

Cork (Glanmire) : Great Southern 4-6-0 No 402 waits to back down to its station to pick up a Dublin express in September 1954

Athlone Shed : Ex-MGW 0-6-0 No 719 in August 1953

Bantry: One time Cork, Bandon & South Coast Railway 4-6-0 tank in July 1952

Railway Closed: Sligo Leitrim & Northern Counties Railway 0-6-4 tank *Lissadell* at Manorhamilton in 1958

Belfast, Queens Quay: Belfast & County Down Railway—large 4-4-2 tank outside the shed in June 1949

Portlaoghise: This Great Southern D2 class No 331 (originated in 1904) was photographed in August 1953. The class, rebuilt with new frames and boilers, continued to do good work until the late 1950s and the end of steam on the CIE

Clonmel: The D3 class was designed in 1907/8 for the Rosslare road. No 334 was photographed in August 1953

Last Survivors: The Atock 650 class of the old Midland Great Western dated from 1893. They were the last 2-4-0s to run in the British Isles. This picture of No 668 was taken at Inchicore, Dublin in 1957

Skibbereen: The F6 class was the 2-4-2 tank version of MacDonnell's 2-4-0 engines of 1873. The F6s dated from 1892 and were used on most Great Southern minor branch lines. No 33 was photographed in July 1952

Portrait at Adelaide (i): Ex-GNR class SG3 0-6-0 newly painted in UTA livery in June 1960

Portrait at Adelaide (ii): Ex-Great Southern 4-6-0 No 800 *Maeve* awaits removal to the Belfast Transport Museum in March 1962

Portrait at Adelaide (iii): Ex-NCC Derby-built 2-6-4 tank No 54 (nicknamed *The Jeeps*) in UTA livery in March 1963

Portrait at Adelaide (iv): Ex-NCC W class Mogul No 91 *The Bush* in July 1957

Portrait at Adelaide (v): Ex-SLNCR 0-6-4 tank *Lough Melvin,* then UTA No 26, in March 1962

Postwar Narrow Gauge at Home: The Welsh Lines

During the course of the War trains continued to operate on all the Welsh narrow gauge lines with the exception of the Vale of Rheidol section of the Great Western Railway. In the main these trains were freight only: indeed it was solely the ancient Talyllyn which bothered to carry passengers at all. It was a pretty sorry picture for the lines were run down and the maintenance carried on, at Boston Lodge, Towyn and Maespoeth was poor indeed, if it existed at all. But there was worse to come. It began at Boston Lodge on the Festiniog Railway.

On August 1, 1946 as the crew of the 0-4-0 *Princess* was coaling her in readiness for her next trip the following week they were approached by the Manager, told the line was closing and given a week's notice. The gorse and saplings which had been growing since the cessation of passenger services in September 1939 were no longer discouraged by the infrequent passage of the slate trains and before long the whole railway took on an air of desolation and decay. Almost two years later the Corris Railway, which had survived just about long enough to be nationalised, also shut up shop. Fortunately the Great Western had re-opened the Vale of Rheidol in the summer of 1945. The Talyllyn had continued to operate through the doggedness of its ageing owner, Sir Henry Haydn Jones. All in all the picture did not seem promising.

It seemed even less so in the summer of 1950 when Sir Haydn died and at the end of the season the ancient *Dolgoch* joined her sister *Talyllyn* to lie cold in the Talyllyn's shed at Towyn, Pendre. But as so often happens when an institution is declining and about to disappear the public was now beginning to take an interest in the Welsh narrow gauge lines and this began in earnest that autumn with the formation of the Talyllyn Railway Preservation Society. Imitation is the sincerest form of flattery and a number of similar schemes has since been launched here and overseas, including one which has spectacularly resurrected the Festiniog itself.

The new life which enthusiasts have brought to these lines can be seen by a glance at the loco sheds concerned. Today a prospering Talyllyn has extended its depot by doubling its size and the adjoining workshop is capable of carrying out anything but the very heaviest repair. The Festiniog shops at Boston Lodge are the epitome of good minor railway workshop practice—there is little in the way of locomotive and rolling stock repair work which cannot be dealt with there. As with the Talyllyn, shed accommodation has been greatly enlarged and additional engines have been acquired. The Rheidol too has changed and its locos are now housed in the old main line shed at Aberystwyth. On all these lines there is an air of activity and progress.

Penrhyn Lady: The narrow gauge was cradled in the Welsh mountains and the Penrhyn Quarry Railway was one of the first to be born. Its steam engines came later and many of them are now preserved in working order. In this picture one of the 'main line' engines *Blanche* (now on the Festiniog Railway) is seen having minor repairs on shed at Bethesda in October 1953

Terrace Engine: *Winifred* was one of the smaller Hunslet engines used for working the quarry terraces. She is seen here outside the workshops at Bethesda in 1953

Charles: Another Penrhyn 'main line' engine, now preserved in the Industrial Railway Museum at Penrhyn Castle. The photograph was taken in 1951

Festiniog Engine (i): Probably the most famous narrow gauge engines of all are the Festiniog's double Fairlies. Two are still working, but *Taliesin* shown in this picture in 1959 has now been renamed *Earl of Merioneth*

Festiniog Engine (ii): *Prince*, built in 1865, is one of the two oldest narrow gauge engines in existence. This engine is still in regular service in the summer season. The scene is Boston Lodge in 1959

Talyllyn Engines (i): The 0-4-2 tank *Talyllyn* (left) was recently entirely rebuilt in her 1865 form. She still shares part of the seasonal service with the newer *Edward Thomas* fitted with a Giesl ejector and thus a very modern engine. Both are shown outside the shed at Towyn in September 1965

Talyllyn Engines (ii): *Douglas*, also shown at Towyn in 1965, was a gift to the Railway from an industrialist. It is also one of the regular engines at work from Towyn to Abergynolwyn in the summer season

Rheidol Engine: The only steam engines now working on British Rail are on its narrow gauge line from Aberystwyth to Devils Bridge. All three are named. Here is No 8 *Llywelyn* at Aberystwyth in July 1957

Welshpool Engine: No 822, *The Earl* stands outside the narrow gauge shed at Welshpool in May 1954. At that time the line was still in BR ownership and relatively busy

Postwar Narrow Gauge: The Irish Lines

On Tuesday January 31, 1961 all operations on the 3ft 0in gauge in Ireland—once the richest narrow gauge territory in these Islands—ceased. That winter evening less than a decade ago the last railcar throbbed its way through the boulder-strewn countryside of County Clare, disgorged its passengers alongside the main line platform at Ennis, and made off quietly to the shed which once housed four different classes of steam locomotives. By this time the West Clare Section of CIE was entirely diesel worked, but even this had not saved it—merely prolonged its operation by something like five years.

The majority of the Irish narrow gauge lines survived the war, but by the early 'fifties few were left. Some, like the Schull & Skibbereen never survived the fuel emergency in 1947, others, like the Tralee & Dingle hung on to life by a single thread (the monthly cattle specials) and others, like the Londonderry & Lough Swilly merely awaited the delivery of lorries and a few road improvements to abandon and go over to road transport. Each line differed considerably in character and each had its own distinct locomotive policy, and what is more each was very amenable. For example, a request to the stationmaster at Skibbereen would always ensure that the loco shed was opened and a conducted tour given. On one occasion even the 0-4-4 tank 6S was specially steamed for photography after the railway had been closed for at least three years. But whether in the South West, West or North West these lines and their engines were fascinating. Tralee would produce the Hunslet 2-6-0 tanks with No 2T always placed with its chimney under a hole in the roof, Ennis had 0-6-2 tanks with trailing and driving wheels all the same size, and the Swilly's shed at Londonderry housed those huge 4-8-4 tanks—so large that it was difficult to believe this was the narrow gauge at all.

The last all-steam line to go was the Cavan & Leitrim section based on Ballinamore. Here the funeral was on March 31, 1959. The last rites were due to begin at 7pm with the departure of the final train to Dromod and this eventually left at 7.38pm with the whole of the passenger stock still able to run. It was double-headed by two ex-Tralee & Dingle engines Nos 4T (Kerr Stuart) and 5T (the Hunslet 2-6-2 tank). The very last train of all—the return working from Dromod, reached Ballinamore at 11.8pm—well over an hour and twenty minutes late, and here almost the whole town turned out. The coaches were left in the platform and as the two engines whistled their eldritch way to the shed a local Councillor harangued the crowd, making frequent references to the undoubted fact that it was the railway which had provided WORK for the populace for so many years.

The closing of the Cavan & Leitrim left only the dieselised West Clare, and the large County Donegal Railway based on Stranorlar—a line where passenger railcars introduced as early as 1931 had prolonged its life for nearly thirty years. But the Donegal still ran steam on its freights and on the odd Bank Holiday special. It used 2-6-4 and 4-6-4 tanks for the purpose. These were shedded at Stranorlar Strabane and Letterkenny; they were then the only red engines in Ireland. It was Stranorlar which ran the last train of all. The final run was made on the last day of 1959 and as the evening drew on and the mails had gone down to Strabane in the railcar No 16, the crowds began to turn up in force at Stranorlar, and it became clear that no railcar could cope with the traffic. So Barney Curran the General Manager decided that the last train would be run by Stranorlar men with steam. This was made up of 2-6-4 tank No 5 *Drumboe*, manned by the McMenamin brothers and consisted of five bogie coaches. When they arrived back on the shed both the brothers were actually in tears, overcome by emotion—for them this really WAS the end, and a lifetime of work on the engines was finished. The next day, New Year's Day 1960, Frank left the service; Jim was kept on as a loader, but as he said—it will never be the same again.

NOTICE
PASSENGERS MUST
CROSS THE LINE BY
THE FOOTBRIDGE

West Clare (i) : During the transition period from steam to diesel in the early 1950s, the 3ft-gauge engines at Ennis made good use of the water tank in the station. 4-6-0 tank No 3C has brought in a train from Kilrush in July 1951

West Clare (ii) : These 4-6-0 tanks were the largest used on this line and were very popular. In the main they were used for the passenger workings leaving the freights to the 0-6-2 tanks. No 7C is standing outside the shed at Ennis in June 1950

Cavan & Leitrim (i) : This section was the last of the narrow gauge lines in Eire to go. It survived until 1958 due almost entirely to the coal traffic from the Arigna mines. Some Arigna slack is loaded into the cab of ex-Tralee & Dingle 2-6-0 tank No 3T in August 1958

Cavan & Leitrim (ii) : Another ex-Dingle engine was 4T, a smaller 2-6-0 tank built by Kerr Stuart, the other T&D locos being Hunslet-built. No 4T is shown here at Ballinamore in August 1956

Tralee & Dingle (i) : Tralee shed was capable of storing four engines and in the old days it also had considerable workshop facilities. The locomotives are 6T, IT, and 2T; July 1950

Tralee & Dingle (ii) : Hunslet 2-6-0 tank No 6T sits on the turntable at Tralee in July 1950

Ballycastle: Sitting outside the shed in May 1949 is No 44, one of the two-cylinder compound 2-4-2 tanks that worked the Ballymena—Ballycastle 3ft-gauge section of the then UTA

Schull and Skibbereen: This section of CIE's narrow gauge closed 'temporarily' in the fuel shortage of 1947, and never reopened though the locomotives stood outside the shed at Skibbereen for several years after. 0-4-4 tank No 6s was photographed in July 1952

County Donegal (i): This was the largest of Ireland's narrow gauge lines. It lasted until the end of 1959. The headquarters and works were at Stranorlar where the 4-6-4 tank *Erne* stands in August 1957

County Donegal (ii): These were the larger CDRJC 4-6-4 tanks—*Alice, Blanche* and *Lydia. Alice* was often seen on Letterkenny branch and is depicted outside the shed there in August 1958

Isle of Man Railway

Like so many railways in Britain and Ireland the lines in the Isle of Man eventually found that road competition was too much for them. Both the Manx Electric and then the Isle of Man Railway itself fell prey, though the former has been rescued by the Manx Government as a tourist attraction. The larger Isle of Man Railway (still steam operated bar two diesel railcars purchased at the sale of the County Donegal Railway) closed in 1965 and it seemed unlikely to rise again, but fate in the form of Lord Ailsa took a hand in 1967. His Lordship came to an agreement with the Railway Company to lease the whole of the system and this, including the traffic-barren Ramsey branch, has been open to tourists during the summer seasons of 1967 and 1968. To those who had experience of running small lines this magnificent gesture showed danger of running before it had walked and one can only hope that the future will bring some consolidation. It would perhaps have been wiser to have concentrated on the Peel line leaving the dreaded Ramsey section and heavily graded south line to Castletown and Port Erin with all its manned level crossings.

But still these have been two excellent years for those who had not seen the line before and the great shed and workshops at Douglas has been full of live steam once more. Virtually all the engines were repainted in the older type light green livery and some of those out of use have even been done, when applicable, in Manx Northern red. These temporary museum pieces were kept at St John's Road shed during the summer months of 1968 and pulled out daily for tourists to look at. They included the sole 0-6-0 tank *Caledonia* and the newer 1926-built 2-4-0 tank *Mannin*. Both the small sheds at Peel and Port Erin have been in use during this period of new management.

Old Management (i): Due to her larger wheelbase the 0-6-0 tank *Caledonia* was rarely used and spent most of her life at the back of the shed at Douglas. In August 1952, she had the snow-plough attached ready for her next anticipated job in the coming winter

Old Management (ii): No 5 *Mona* backs down to the shed at Peel in June 1956

New Management (i) and (ii) : Inside the shed at Douglas
in July 1968 are Nos 8 *Fenella* and 11 *Maitland*. Both
had been in steam and are painted in the new light green
livery

New Management (iii): No 8 *Maitland,* shining in her
new livery, stands in the almost traditional spot alongside
the rusty wheels outside Douglas shed in July 1968

New Management (iv): No 12
Hutchinson waits for the morning train
to Peel in July 1968   [*C. M. Whitehouse*

Tyseley Shed—Men and Machines

My first memories of Tyseley go back nearly forty years—engines on the old steam depot were easily seen from the main Birmingham to Warwick road, and on visits to friends in Warwick I always tried to persuade reluctant parents to make that slight detour to see just what was standing outside. Sometimes these pleas were successful and one could peer through the iron railings to see *Lady of Lynne*, *Saint Helena*, *County Wicklow*, *County of Somerset* and the dozens of unnamed engines unworthy of putting in the notebook.

But it has been the last ten years which have seen the highlights—and of course the sadness of departing steam. During the 'fifties the great thing was to have a ride on one of Tyseley's more interesting turns—the nightly Swindon Parcels which ran via Stratford, Gloucester and up the notorious Sapperton bank. This was generally a Hall turn but every now and again, if we talked to Mr Davies the Shedmaster nicely, he would phone Wolverhampton Stafford Road for us and borrow a Star—often 4056 *Princess Margaret*. This was also one of the engines used for the annual SLS pilgrimage to Swindon and what a run we had with her going down via Worcester and the Old Worse and Worse over Campden Bank. The best of these trips was in the year we had 6018; 1963. Officially all the Kings had gone months earlier but as this excursion had been advertised with a King she was kept for us and made her last passenger run with the special. Tyseley had her for a week to run her in and we ran her on the evening locals to Leamington—what a week that was too.

Then we bought 4555—a Great Western small-wheeled 2-6-2 tank. The original idea was that she would go to David Garnock's Middleton Railway at Leeds but somehow or other she came to Tyseley. She was repainted and tidied up in the 'factory' there just before it closed and Tom Field the present Depot Superintendent—then using the humbler title of 'shedmaster', had her out on some of the locals and on the trip goods. One day she was shunting at Leamington when the down 'Pines' came in with a faulty Hall. No 4555 was put on the front and ran the 22 miles to Birmingham in 28 minutes including the formidable Hatton bank of 1 in 100.

Later, when we bought 7029 *Clun Castle* and got to know Tom Field and the lads better, we found a comradeship which is still tangible evidence of how teamwork can work wonders. Nothing has been too much trouble and in their own time Tyseley men have looked after the engine as if it were their own—anyone from Tom through Jock Nicholson, his Mechanical Foreman, and on to Graham Smith the Boilersmith have helped out with advice and practical skills. When 7029 limped back from Birkenhead in March 1967 with a thread stripped from her right hand outside valve spindle the valve was taken out and made new within three days, and later when we purchased 5593 *Kolhapur* we were allowed to use the diesel depot whilst we put a new smokebox on her.

Now Tyseley has no BR steam, but tucked away beyond the old roundhouse there is still steam to be found. Here, with coal and watering facilities the old GW coaling stage has been converted into a modern depot for *Clun Castle* and *Kolhapur*, and Tyseley men are there in their off duty hours to help maintain them. Such is the interest that has been engendered that at an open day in the autumn of 1968 some 15,000 people paid to see the whole of the depot, old and new.

Sunshine and Shadow: Steam is still supreme in June 1953

On the Table: In June 1953 the shed st
possessed the old hand turntable complete
boarded over

Up from London: In the early 1960s 61xx 2-6-
tanks were replaced by dmus on the Paddingto
suburban services, but No 6134 had found h
way north to Birmingham by June 1953

Conversation Piece: An ex-ROD 2-8-0 is flanked by two examples from standard Great Western classes in May 1954

Stand Pipe: An essential part of the shed scene

Fitters' Bench: Far from ideal working conditions in the old steam shed

The Last Star: No 4056 *Princess Margaret* inside the passenger shed in June 1956. Note the cleanliness of both engine and shed

Suburban Locos: Two standard 2-6-2 tanks and a 53xx all used on the Leamington locals sit in the steam shed in September 1963

The Last County: No 1011 *County of Chester* being prepared for her last run on an enthusiasts' special

The LM Takes Over: During the last years of steam, ex-LMS engines predominated at Tyseley. Here is 2-8-0 No 48122 in April 1966

The Great Marquess: In March 1967, this preserved ex-LNER K4 class 2-6-0 called in at Tyseley for a few days. During that time she was the subject of an oil painting; the artist—Terence Cuneo. Steam was finished in Birmingham then from BR point of view

Postwar Narrow Gauge in Europe

The notable thing about the narrow gauge in Europe is not how much has disappeared but how much still remains. But in spite of this, the mortality continues to mount year by year. Here the concept of the narrow gauge is quite different from the little lines found in our Islands and where railways are being kept at all they are becoming rapidly dieselised both by passenger railcars and new locomotives. In France there is now only one narrow gauge common carrier that even keeps a steam engine in reserve—the PO Corrèze system based on Tulle. During 1967/8 there was great slaughter and the two finest lines of all, the Réseau Breton and the CFD du Vivarais both closed.

Austria keeps the flag flying at Jenbach with both the Zillertalbahn and the splendid and preposterous Achenseebahn with its peculiar rack engines; whilst in Styria in the south east the Provincial Government still operates some pretty steam engines amidst mountain scenery. Germany has practically nothing left: Scandinavia is now barren, apart from two preserved lines in Norway: only in part of Spain do steam-worked narrow-gauge lines still run in fair number, and in Portugal where several splendid lines survive in full glory, with few railcars and no diesel locomotives whatever.

It is to the south east into the Balkans that one must go to find the finest narrow gauge steam of all but this too is on the decline and closures have begun. The Yugoslavs still operate a somewhat truncated but still comparatively large 2ft 6in gauge network by steam. The most fascinating section of all is without doubt the line from Lapcavic and Cacak over the mountains via Titovo Uzice and Visegrad to Sarajevo. This section is still worked by 2-8-2s and 0-8-2s with trains of up to ten corridor coaches, though certain services are now being operated by modern railcars: sad for the steam enthusiast, but admittedly vastly more comfortable and faster. But the sheds at Cacak, Visegrad and Sarajevo are still full of steam, with the engines well cared for—some are even adorned with polished brass shell cases containing flowers in addition to the wings and red star on their smokeboxes. The other well-known line from Sarajevo to Dubrovnik has been standard gauged as far as Capljina and here too most of the through services and connections are multiple unit worked. In spite of that, for those holidaying in the delightful Dubrovnik area the shed there is well worth a visit. There is still a fair number of other 2ft 6in gauge lines, including one with a steam-worked rack section, between Traunik and Jajce.

The Greek narrow gauge is still in quite good shape with the Peloponnesus line still intact though more dieselised than one might wish. The three gauges and four rails at Volos on the east coast still survive and these lines are well worth visiting. In particular the 2ft gauge line up to Mileae should be looked at—sadly the Germans only left it with three locomotives and the traffic is slight.

PO Corrèze: Down beyond Clermont Ferrand at Tulle stands the headquarters of this metre gauge line. Officially there is now no steam, but an 0-4-4-0 Mallet tank is still kept in reserve. The picture of No 101 was taken in May 1965

The depot at Argentat: Steam was still in use on the freight and mixed trains in 1959

Reseau Breton (i): Carhaix was the centre of a five pointed metre-gauge star. There one could once see steam in action most of the day including the 0-6-6-0 compound Mallet tanks. No E 413 comes on to the shed in September 1966

Reseau Breton (ii): E 414 has her smoke box ash removed at Carhaix in August 1965

Côtes du Nord (i): Corpet Louvet tank No 36 loads up with briquettes at St Brieuc in June 1955

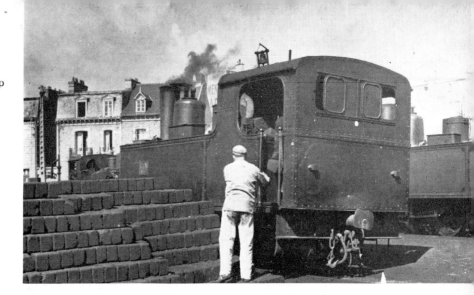

Côtes du Nord (ii): Paimpol was the outer terminus of the last remnant of this once extensive network. Here, Corpet Louvet tank No 39 sits crab-like on the turntable after bringing in an enthusiasts' excursion

Cotes du Nord (iii): The hub of the system was at St Brieuc where red 0-6-0 tanks Nos 39 and 36 wait for their day's work in June 1955

Vivarais (i): Franco-Belge 0-6-6-0 Mallet tank No 413 sits outside the shed at Le Cheylard in July 1964

Vivarais (ii): Swiss-built Mallet tank No 401 backs off the turntable at St Agiève in July 1964. This line, closed in 1968, used steam for its freight services until the mid 1960s

Austria (i): A Krauss 0-6-2 tank sizzles outside its shed at Salzburg on the late Salzkammergut Lokalerbahn in August 1956

Austria (ii): Zillertalbahn 0-6-0 tank moves off the shed at Mayerhofen in September 1961

Switzerland: Brienz-Rothornbahn rack tank No 1 waits outside her shed at Brienz in August 1962

Sicily: A 0-6-0 rack tank (No R370) stands at Calabria in May 1954

Greece : Two of the 2-6-0 tanks used on the Milae line stand outside the narrow gauge shed at Volos in October 1964

Czechoslovakia : A Hungarian-built 0-8-0 tank No U45 903 at its depot on the forestry line (750mm) at Liptovsky Hiadok in June 1967

Yugoslavia (i): Engines of the Samobor railway (now completely diesel) at Zagreb in the summer of 1956

Yugoslavia (ii): A 0-6-4 rack tank standing disused on Dubrovnik shed in August 1968

116

Yugoslavia (iii) : One of the standard 760mm 0-8-2 locos No 83 042 waits for coal at Cacak in August 1968

Yugoslavia (iv) : These 2-8-2s used mainly for heavy passenger work on the 760 mm lines were built in Budapest in the 1930s. No 85 036 simmers at Cacak on an August morning in 1968

The Declining Years—Great Western Lines

The last depot in old GW territory to run GW steam on principal express trains was Worcester; it was presided over by Harry Cureton and its engines not only did the job well but looked well into the bargain. At the same time the original 'Old Worse & Worse' works at Worcester were still in being ably ministered by Don Green. Between them the two men saw to it that a failure on the Paddington train was rare indeed.

The end really came in 1964 when the Hymeks began to arrive in some force but even then the 5.15pm down from Paddington was often Castle-hauled. Knowing that the end was near I would often come home from London to Birmingham on that train, usually with a footplate pass, and what runs we had. The route itself was worth taking for its history and scenic value. It was right away Oxford via the main line and Reading with stops beyond at Kingham, Moreton in Marsh and Evesham where we would always pass the up evening fast from Hereford and Worcester, inevitably Castle-hauled. But the best bit of all was coming down Campden bank towards Honeybourne where there was always the temptation to try to do the 'ton'—and Harry's engines could do it too.

The highlight was March and April 1964 for this was while Gerry Fiennes was GM at Paddington and he was prepared to have a go. This is just what he did when Ian Allan suggested a *City of Truro* commemorative special from London to Plymouth and back in May of that year—to be the last really high speed trip with steam to the west. The attempt was to beat *City of Truro's* timing from Plymouth to Bristol and on the Bristol to London leg to do 100mph. The problem was to find the engines to do it and these when picked were tried out on the Paddington–Worcester trains and *what* evenings those were: holding on for dear life with the rough bouncing *Pendennis Castle* but making the pace just the same. The engines which I can remember hitting at least this speed down Campden were 4079, 5054, 7027 and 7029.

But the Indian Summer was soon over and steam in the Western Region finished entirely after January 1, 1966. No 7029 *Clun Castle* which beat *City of Truro's* timing that wonderful day in May 1964 was kept to the end; she was among the last of the Western Region's steam engines to go. Her last days were spent at Gloucester where she was used on the odd fast when needed to replace a diesel and on enthusiasts' specials. She was fortunately bought privately and is now kept as a live museum piece at Tyseley in Birmingham—an old Great Western shed.

During the last years of steam some of the old Great Western system fell into LMR hands including the lines north of Banbury and on the Cambrian Coast. By mid-1966 all Great Western steam engines had been taken out of service bar one or two 57xx tanks left for a few months to work the old Halesowen Basin branch. In the last year or so of steam at ex-GWR sheds now under LM control (such as Banbury, Tyseley, Croes Newydd, Birkenhead and Machynlleth) the ex-LMS and standard locomotives which remained were mostly black and grimy. Machynlleth did keep its standard class 4 4-6-0s reasonably clean and in the last summer, and the winter of 1966/7, enthusiasts from all parts regularly went down to the shed to clean the engines for the 'Cambrian Coast Express'—they even provided them with newly painted front number plates made of wood. So steam on the Western went out not unsung, finishing with the remarkable weekend of March 4/5, 1967, when the last run of the 'Cambrian Coast' coincided with the end of the Paddington–Birkenhead through service and the three specials worked north of Birmingham by *Clun Castle* and *Pendennis Castle*.

Banbury: A class 5 and a Castle, both in appalling external condition are serviced on a June evening in 1965

Birkenhead: An unknown BR standard
9F 2-10-0 waits for her evening's
work on March 4, 1967, the last day
of through working from Shrewsbury,
Birmingham and London

[*C. M. Whitehouse*

Bristol: In May 1964 Ian Allan Ltd in conjunction with the Western Region ran a 'last' high speed special from Paddington to Plymouth and back with their Castle class 4-6-0s. The final leg was hauled by No 5054 *Earl of Ducie* seen here at Bath Coal Depot

Machynlleth: During the last year of steam, only BR standard engines worked the ex-Cambrian lines. In the main there were the class 4 4-6-0s similar to No 75004 which is seen here in September 1966

The Declining Years—LNER Lines

It was Glasgow (St Rollox) and Aberdeen (Ferryhill) sheds that saw the finish of LNER express steam. After the GN/NE main line became finally dieselised, the A4 streamlined Pacifics were sent up to the old Caledonian line from Glasgow to Aberdeen to work out their lives; among them were *William Whitelaw, Union of South Africa, Kingfisher* and *Bittern*. No 60019 *Bittern* was the last engine to go through the works at Darlington and they made a good job of her. In addition to this team of A4s there was an odd man out—the A2 Pacific *Blue Peter*. Such was the fame of these engines that three of them, *Union of South Africa, Bittern* and *Blue Peter* have been saved for posterity by private preservation.

Although the last expresses worked by LNER power were Glasgow to Aberdeen trains, other LNER engines still abounded in Scotland and in the North East of England. Dundee, Tay Bridge shed in the early autumn of 1967 had a variety of LNER classes including an A2, at least one V2 class 2-6-2, B1 4-6-0s and some North British 0-6-0s. Bradford, Leeds and the West Riding saw the odd B1 until as late as autumn 1966. The last official steam-hauled train out of Hull was also with a B1 though this was on April 16, 1967. All in all the summer and autumn of 1967 saw the end of regular steam in the North Eastern Area. Among the last to go were strangely enough two pre-grouping classes—the 1913 Raven-designed Q6 class 0-8-0 and the NE J27 class 0-6-0. The Q6s could be found at such sheds as Hartlepool, Sunderland and Tyne Dock whilst the J27s also inhabited this part of the world in addition to North and South Blyth.

The last indigenous steam engines to run over the old LNER main line have been two classes of pacific—Alan Pegler's A3 No 4472 *Flying Scotsman*, shedded at Doncaster under a private contract; and for a short while in 1967, the restored A4 No 4498 *Sir Nigel Gresley* at that time temporarily based at Crewe together with No 60019 *Bittern* also privately owned and kept at York. There was also an interloper at York and Peterborough sheds for approximately six weeks during August, September and October 1967. This was *Clun Castle* which though privately owned, was borrowed by the Eastern Region to run a series of special excursions from King's Cross.

Aberdeen: The last main line passenger engines to work express services were the Gresley A4s based on Glasgow and Aberdeen. The pictures on the accompanying pages show No 60024 *Kingfisher* on Aberdeen shed during the final week of operation in September 1966

End of the Line: In September 1966, the last of Gresley's mixed traffic 2-6-2s of class V2 were stationed at Dundee. No 60836 was on no preservation list for the original engine *Green Arrow* had been kept for official preservation. She has been restored to LNER colours and is at present in the old roundhouse at Leicester

North Eastern Survivor: The last steam engines to survive in the north east were, strangely enough, pre-grouping classes in the J27 0-6-0 and the 1913 Raven-designed Q6 0-8-0. They lasted until November 1967. The J27s were found at North and South Blyth whilst the Q6 class joined them at Tyne Dock, Sunderland and Hartlepool. No 63395 was photographed at Tyne Dock in September 1967

The Declining Years—Southern Lines

The former Southern Railway's main line from London to Bournemouth, like the Norfolk & Western on the other side of the Atlantic, became a mecca for steam enthusiasts long after the diesels reigned elsewhere on fast passenger work. Because the Southern Region stayed with steam whilst awaiting main line electrification, the summer of 1967 still saw Oliver Bulleid's Pacifics heading boat trains to Southampton and Pullmans to Bournemouth, and sheds at Nine Elms, Eastleigh and Bournemouth still maintained them. Even though, in the last months up to the finale in July 1967, most of them were in a pretty run down condition they did their job remarkably well and train timing enthusiasts had a few glorious weeks. Speeds of 90mph in each direction were far from rare and on an up run in June 1967 No 35028 *Clan Line* ran from Southampton to Eastleigh in nine minutes when loaded to 10 coaches, and following a long relaying restriction in the Shawford area accelerated the whole way up the bank passing Roundwood at 66mph. The engine then proceeded to give a splendid display east of Basingstoke to arrive at Waterloo $13\frac{3}{4}$ minutes early in a net time of $75\frac{1}{2}$ minutes. This feat was equalled on several other occasions and it is true to say that due to the efforts of the enthusiastic staff of the sheds concerned the general level of steam running between Southampton and Waterloo was rarely higher than in those last months of April, May and June 1967.

Up to the end of the Southern's steam there were standard 2-6-4 tanks acting as station pilots at Waterloo and number of standard class 4 and 5 4-6-0s and 2-6-0s was still at work as well.

The other section of the Southern to stay steam until 1967 was the Isle of Wight—the ancient and diminutive O2 class 0-4-4 tanks remaining until the total closure of the Island's system, bar the London tube stock operated-section from Ryde to Shanklin. The main shed and works were at Ryde, St John's and the old ladies, still in lined out black livery, did their work well—it speaks highly of the care lavished on them at depot and works when one remembers that at the end no engine was less than 74 years old. The solid brass nameplates had been removed from the engines to avoid theft and vandalism by so-called enthusiasts early in 1966 and one of the last surprises was the cheaper but distinctive plates made in the last months and fitted to the engines still in use. Older railway enthusiasts will recall that the Isle of Wight Railway always kept its stock and locos in the best possible manner and this was a tradition which Ryde continued until steam finally finished—a proud record lasting just on 102 years.

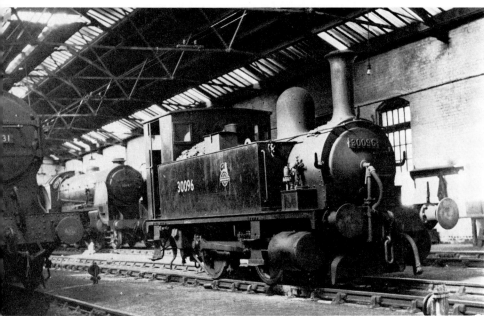

Eastleigh: Though the South Western classes did not last until the very end of Southern steam (1967) they hung on at Southampton for longer than their counterparts in other regions. Eastleigh shed itself kept on until the end, and to the finish it housed ex-Southern engines in the form of Bulleid Pacifics. The pictures on this page were taken in June 1958: King Arthur class 4-6-0 No 30791; inside the shed a dock 0-4-0 tank No 30096, and T9 class 4-4-0 No 30117

Bournemouth (i):
Standard BR 2-6-4
tanks and a new diesel
electric painted blue
and yellow stand out-
side the shed in June
1967

Bournemouth (ii):
An ex-LSWR M7 class
0-4-4 tank on the shed
in August 1956

Bournemouth (iii):
One of the last survivors of the rebuilt version of the Bulleid Pacific, No 34004, moves on to the depot on a June afternoon in 1962

Bournemouth (iv):
Being serviced on the shed in June 1967 are Standard 4-6-0 No 73092 and an unknown BR 2-6-4 tank. In the distance Bulleid Pacific No 34004 enters the yard.

The Declining Years—LMS Lines

Steam officially finished its working life on British Rail on Sunday, August 4, 1968, although it lingered on for a week until the last BR steam train to end all ran on the following Sunday, August 11. The final steam sheds were Carnforth, Rose Grove and Lostock Hall and the final classes (bar the preserved Britannia No 70013 *Oliver Cromwell* specially kept back for the August 11 junketing) were ex-LMS class 5 4-6-0s and class 8 2-8-0s plus some BR Standard class 5 and class 4 4-6-0s.

The LM Region hung on to its steam locomotives for over a year longer than the Southern and there were still one or two steam passenger workings right up to the last day—during that twelve months enthusiasts must have used up miles of film and recording tape. One of the highlights of the summer of 1967 was the Saturday workings of two Scottish expresses from Leeds to Carlisle; these were regularly hauled by Holbeck's last two Jubilee's, 45562 *Alberta* and 45593 *Kolhapur*, and BR must have collected a few hundred pounds from the tape recorder fans alone. Both '62 and '93 were in fair fettle and Tommy Greaves the Assistant Maintenance Engineer at Leeds was an enthusiast so the runs were pretty good, and Holbeck even turned out *Alberta* for use on a Royal train that autumn. Two of the ex-Holbeck engines—a 'Black Five' No 45428 and No 45593 *Kolhapur* have survived and are now at Tyseley shed.

Other ex-LMS sheds which survived until the close of 1967 were Tebay with its bankers for Shap (BR class 4 4-6-0s) and Carlisle, Kingmoor, the latter having on its roster the majority of the remaining Britannia Pacifics. In fact one of these, No 70021 *Morning Star*, must have worked the last regular express turn for its class—the morning Glasgow–Manchester train from Preston on December 28, 1967. The sheds in the Manchester and Liverpool area hung on until the summer of 1968, Newton Heath being the last to go. It was a sad sight to walk round the depot the Monday after steam finished with all the engines lying dead and fitters removing the more obvious brass fittings in case of vandalism and theft.

A visit to Carnforth on August 2 was almost as bad though a good number of engines was still at work—most of which had tenders marked in chalk—'do not coal'. I rode down to Morecambe that sunny afternoon on the footplate of a grimy LMS 'Black Five' and came back to Preston with the Lostock Hall breakdown train which had been picking up some bogie tankers which had come off the road. We changed crews at Lancaster and as the first men left they pulled a face—'It'll not be quite the same' they said. I left Jack Sedgebeer, the Lostock Hall depot super, at Preston—he and his men had been out for nearly 24 hours with the crane—just another job in its way but they will certainly remember the penultimate day of steam.

It was Lostock Hall that provided the engines for the two last steam passenger trains on British Rail—(it also provided engines for the specials on the following two Sundays but that was not quite the same somehow). The engines were both LMS 'Fives'—45212 worked the 20.48 to Blackpool South and 45318 the 21.25 to Liverpool Exchange. To say that these trains were crowded was an understatement—the corridors were packed, reminiscent of a Sunday night train during the war—so full was it that many photographers and recorders could do nothing in the jam—one enterprising gentleman had locked himself in a toilet and no doubt tied his microphone to the ventilating grid. At Liverpool they sang 'Auld Lang Syne'. It was all over.

Leeds, Holbeck (i): 2-6-4 tank No 42699 waits for water before taking up station pilot duties in September 1966

Leeds, Holbeck (ii): One of the last of her class, Jubilee 4-6-0 No 45593 *Kolhapur* comes off the table ready for her day's work in September 1966

Leeds, Farnley Junction (i): Jubilee class 4-6-0 No 45647 *Sturdee* on the triangle outside the shed in September 1966

Leeds, Farnley Junction (ii): BR standard 2-10-0 No 92048 shortly after arriving at the depot; June 1966

Leeds, Holbeck: A North Eastern Q6 class 0-8-0
stands out of use in September 1966

Leeds, Farnley Junction (iii): Jubilees *Alberta* and
Sturdee ready to go off shed in September 1966

Saltley Shed (i) & (ii) : This was the last depot in the Birmingham Division to remain open for steam and during the final months, conditions were pretty primitive. The stud consisted of ex-LMS 'Black Fives' and 8Fs plus BR Standard 9Fs, including the odd Crosti-boilered locomotive. Engines in two of the three round houses stood Irish fashion under a roof with no covering

Tebay and the Last Banker:
The new diesel depot at
Carlisle was completed slightly ahead of schedule and
officially all steam shedded
there, including most of the
remaining Britannias, came
out of service at the close of
1967. Tebay lasted for a
few weeks more but when
steam up Shap finally came
to an end, the last inhabitants
of the shed were BR Standard
class 4 4-6-0s

Carnforth—The Very End:
When steam finally finished
on BR there were three
depots serving steam locomotives—Carnforth, Lostock
Hall and Rose Grove. Officially, Sunday, August 4 was
the end, but 70013 *Oliver
Cromwell* remained at Carnforth until August 11 to
run BR's final farewell special.
During the last year of steam,
Carnforth shed had many
interesting visitors including
one of the two surviving
Jubilees, 45562 *Alberta,* in
September 1967

Redundancy: Men and Machines at Carlisle

The Industrial Scene—Coal and Quarry

There are comparatively few railway students who have interested themselves in the locomotives of the private lines which abound in industry throughout Great Britain. Those who have studied this vast army of different makes, types, classes and colours of engine have reaped a rich harvest both on the standard and narrow gauges. The better known lines have usually been owned either by collieries or quarries but manufacturing industry has had some gems. Some of these but not many survive today.

There were of course some, for the want of a better term, 'fringe' industrial railway students—the knowledgeable few who sought the retired main line locomotives sold out of service by the Big Company and who visited industrial sheds to meet the ageing veterans. Even today there are a few of these engines still at work in this manner, examples being two classes of ex-GWR pannier tanks, the normal 57xx in South Wales and the later Hawksworth outside cylinder 0-6-0 tanks of the 15xx class at Coventry. Until 1968 there was even a North Stafford 0-6-2 tank working from the NCB depot at Walkden in Lancashire and until 1950 ICI had an ex-LNWR 0-4-0 saddle tank. Other standard gauge lines that were well worth seeing for their immaculately kept engines were Bass, Ratcliffe & Gretton at Burton, and the old Hartley Main Colliery which ran some long-boilered outside-framed tender engines.

Better known in recent years have been the quarry railways which were almost all narrow gauge. This interest has almost certainly arisen from the successful preservation of the Festiniog and Talyllyn railways, the latter having a narrow gauge museum at its Towyn terminus. The narrow gauge preservers having consolidated their railways and built up their traffic, have of necessity had to look for additional motive power and some of this has been obtained from now redundant quarry locos. For example, the Festiniog has acquired two of the late Penrhyn Quarry Railway's 'main line' engines *Linda* and *Blanche*—the third of these engines having found a haven among other narrow and standard gauge locomotives in the Industrial Railway Museum contained in the grounds of Penrhyn Castle near Bangor. Other Welsh quarry engines can be seen in steam from time to time in the Dowty Railway Collection at Ashchurch, Gloucestershire, and at Alan Bloom's Bressingham Hall near Diss in Norfolk. The Bressingham collection also contains the 0-4-4-0 Garratt (standard gauge) from the NCB Baddesley Colliery in Warwickshire and a low-slung 0-4-0 saddle tank from Beckton Gas Works.

But there are still many industrial engines still hard at work and visits to their depots can usually be arranged. Most of the NCB locomotives tend to be the 'Austerity' 0-6-0 saddle tanks but there are still plenty of working engines built by Andrew Barclay, Avonside, Bagnall, Black Hawthorn, and companies through the alphabet to the Yorkshire Engine Co Ltd. Most of the lines are standard gauge but there are a few narrow gauge survivors still in operation—one example being the apple green engines of the Bowater Company at Sittingbourne. The study of industrial locomotives is an exacting science and the location of a particular engine sometimes difficult to find for, particularly with the NCB, locomotives tend to move from line to line. For those who wish to make a study of this fascinating subject I cannot do better than to recommend the series of pocket books on Industrial Locomotives issued by the Industrial Locomotive Section of the Birmingham Locomotive Club. These booklets are extremely accurate, cover the whole country, and contain full information on the locomotives concerned and their whereabouts.

Rawnsley (i): This unique 2-4-0 tank named *Birch* was a 'home-made' product by the Cannock & Rugeley Collieries in 1888. It lived until 1956 and was photographed in June 1954

Rawnsley (ii): The 0-6-0 saddle tank *Marquis* came from Lilleshall Iron Co who built her in 1868. She was scrapped within only three years of her centenary and was photographed in October 1964

LBSC Engine: Somewhat altered by a rather ugly Rawnsley chimney, this ex-Brighton 0-6-0 tank is now preserved at Hednesford, Staffs. The picture shows her in Cannock & Rugeley Collieries' livery in September 1947

Giesl Engine: Although the Giesl ejector proved itself in Europe to be a most efficient device it was not adopted by BR. Some of the NCB engines were, however, fitted as this 0-6-0 tank at Atherstone in June 1959

Walkden (i) : The last of the North Stafford tanks was the 0-6-2 *Sir Robert*. This engine survived until the closure of the depot and was photographed there in April 1967

Walkden (ii) : This depot in Lancashire housed a varied and interesting series of locomotives until it was closed in the summer of 1968. In its last years it housed ex-Ministry of Supply 0-6-0 saddle tanks fitted with differing types of coal saving devices such as the Giesl ejector and the last surviving ex-North Stafford Railway 0-6-2 tank

Warwickshire Quarry: This Bagnall 2ft 6in gauge 0-6-0 tank was photographed at its home, Jee's Hartshill Granite Quarries, Nuneaton, in October 1952. The engine is gone, but most of the track survived to be re-laid on the Talyllyn Railway

Caernarvon Quarry: The Dinorwic Quarry, like the Penrhyn, ran its own 'main line' railway (4ft gauge) from face to port. Here is one of the larger engines, *Amalthaea*, in August 1958

Western Survivor: The NCB at Coventry acquired three of the Hawksworth outside cylinder pannier tanks. This picture was taken in 1966 and, at the time of writing, these engines (painted red) are still at work

Coal Board Garrett: This 0-4-0+0-4-0 survived at Baddesley Colliery, Warwickshire, until 1968 when it was acquired by Alan Bloom for preservation at Bressingham. The photograph shows the engine in August 1965

Preserved Steam

Even though steam is now officially dead on British Rail there is still quite a number of locomotives which are very much alive. These range from engines on the narrow gauge lines in Wales, through those on the preserved ex-BR branch lines, to such giants as *Flying Scotsman, Sir Nigel Gresley* and *Clun Castle*.

The idea of live railway and steam preservation was born in October 1950 when a group of people met in the Imperial Hotel, Birmingham and founded the Talyllyn Railway Preservation Society, and from this small beginning other lines have been saved. The next was the better-known Festiniog Railway with its ancient Fairlie 0-4-4-0s, to be followed by the one time GWR-owned Welshpool & Llanfair line. Then came the standard gauge branches led by the Bluebell Railway in Sussex and followed by the Keighley & Worth Valley in Yorkshire and the Dart Valley in Devon. All these lines possess active and historic steam locomotives and they are well worth a visit.

But it was Alan Pegler who really did the trick. He and two of his colleagues persuaded the Eastern Region of BR to bring the two ex-GN Atlantics out of retirement in York Museum in 1953. No one who watched or rode behind Ivatt Atlantic No 62822 as she made her last journey (as the sole survivor of her class) from King's Cross to Doncaster on November 26, 1950, ever thought they would see one of these old ladies at work again. Alan Pegler, Trevor Bailey and Leslie Smith proved them wrong—they ran the first two chartered specials behind preserved locomotives and covered their costs to boot—including the £1,000 which had to be added to the cost of tickets to cover the restoration of the engines.

This, then, was the beginning of the story; Pegler's next move was to rescue and restore as near as possible to her LNER condition the A3 Pacific *Flying Scotsman* and the rest of that story is too well known to repeat here. Suffice it to say that this engine has made money for BR as well as giving joy to its owner and thousands of enthusiasts. The next engines to be acquired for similar tasks were two Swindon-built Castle class 4-6-0s, Nos 4079 *Pendennis Castle* and 7029 *Clun Castle* —these engines worked several specials during 1966/7 including the last train from Birmingham to Birkenhead by steam in March 1967. *Clun Castle* was lent to the Eastern Region in the autumn of 1967 for a series of successful excursions. She is kept at Tyseley depot, Birmingham, alongside ex-LMS No 5593 *Kolhapur* and both engines are steamed regularly. *Pendennis Castle* is at Didcot in Berkshire.

Other privately owned locomotives used for special excursions on BR metals include Lord Garnock's K4 class 2-6-0, No 3442 *The Great Marquess* at present at Neville Hill Shed, Leeds, and two ex-LNER A4 Pacifics, No 4498 *Sir Nigel Gresley* and 60019 *Bittern*. The former engine was put through Crewe works at great expense during the early part of 1967 and is restored to her LNER garter blue lining. *Bittern* is still in BR green and was the last of her class to be shopped. No 4498 is at present on Coal Board property and No 60019 at York.

So it is that within a period of nearly 20 years the seed of steam preservation as a living thing has been sown and has prospered. The Welsh lines are now thriving viable concerns as are the ex-BR branches and they form a valuable part of our country's tourist business. Alan Pegler's adventures with the GN Atlantics and his subsequent acquisition of *Flying Scotsman* have also proved that this type of venture when responsibly organised can be a sound commercial proposition—seats on *Flying Scotsman* specials are today at a premium and in September 1968 some 15,000 people paid 7/6d to come to an open day at Tyseley depot. The Ivatt Atlantics may seem dead in their Museum at York, but maybe even they still only sleep again.

Inspection at Swindon: The first engine to be purchased by the author and his associates was ex-GWR small-wheeled 2-6-2 tank No 4555, seen here at Swindon in the autumn of 1963. To the right of the photograph is Mr R Hanks, one time Chairman of the WR Board

Overhauled at Worcester: Three of the tank engines eventually to be owned by the Dart Valley Railway were overhauled at Worcester works before being sent to Devon. This photograph shows Nos 4555 (in background) and 1420 at Worcester in July 1965

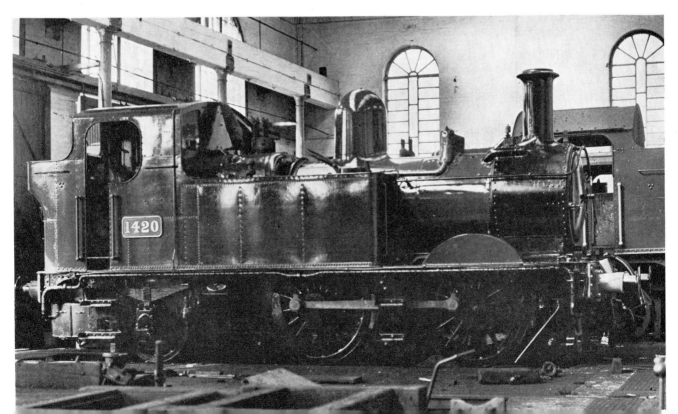

Pendennis Castle (i): The first Castle to be purchased for private preservation was No 4079, a true Great Western engine. She is seen here at Chester on March 3, 1967 having worked one of the two special trains from London and Birmingham to mark the end of the through service from Paddington to Chester and Birkenhead

Pendennis Castle (ii): In March 1967 No 4079 paid a short visit to Tyseley shed, Birmingham, to have her picture painted by Terence Cuneo alongside her British Railways-built sister, *Clun Castle*

Clun Castle (i): On May 4, 1964, No 7029 was used to haul a special fast excursion from Plymouth to Bristol. On this journey she set up what is believed to be a record time for the journey by steam. She is seen here still in BR service in Worcester Shed in April 1966

Clun Castle (ii): After purchase for private preservation, 7029 was overhauled and repainted in the livery in which she emerged from Swindon in 1950, but with the insignia 'Great Western' on her tender at the express wish of Swindon men. In summer 1967, this engine hauled a series of special trains culminating in a very successful visit to the Eastern Region. She is seen here at Banbury shed in July 1967 whilst running trials for her visit to Peterborough

Worth Valley: Painted NER apple green, but still keeping her BR No 69023, *Joem* is kept at Haworth—the headquarters of the Keighley & Worth Valley Light Railway. She was photographed in April 1968

Bluebell: The only surviving ex-GWR 'Dukedog', No 3217, complete with 'Castle' nameplates, sits outside the shed at Sheffield Park in July 1966

Gresley A4: During 1967, No 4498 was put through Crewe Works for an extensive overhaul after being purchased privately. She is painted Garter Blue and was used for some months on enthusiasts' excursions. This photograph was taken in York shed in August 1967

Engines at Leeds: Lord Garnock's K4 class 2-6-0 No 3442 *The Great Marquess* alongside a preserved ex-GER 0-6-2 tank at Neville Hill in September 1966

A4 at Carlisle: *Sir Nigel Gresley* stands under the coaling stage on her inaugural trip after restoration, April 1967

A4 at York: A second A4 No 60019 *Bittern* has also been purchased and has run several excursions. She is still, at the time of writing, housed at York, where this picture was taken in August 1968. Last of the Ferryhill Pacifics, she was the star performer on the Glasgow—Aberdeen expresses before her sale into private ownership

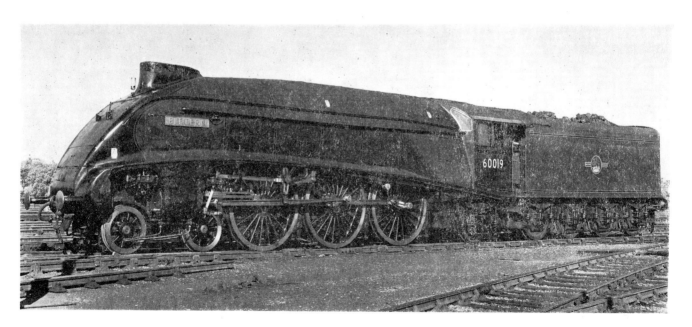

Jubilee at Tyseley (i) : Ex-LMS No 5593 *Kolhapur* was one of the last of her class to remain in service. She lasted (at Holbeck shed, Leeds) until October 1967. She has been purchased and fully restored both mechanically and externally by '7029 Clun Castle Ltd.'. Her nameplates had been sold earlier by BR and this picture was taken shortly before replacements were fitted in May 1968

Jubilee at Tyseley (ii) : *Kolhapur* stands outside her new home at Tyseley in July 1968

Museum Engines

British Railways' collection of Transport Relics is pretty vast. Not only does it include the locomotives and rolling stock in the huge museum at Clapham, but there are also excellent regional displays at York and Swindon. Clapham contains the largest number of exhibits and these are extremely well displayed—they cover virtually the whole lifetime of steam engines in this country from the ancient *Coppernob* to Gresley's record-breaking A4 *Mallard*. The York museum contains locomotives and relics mainly appertaining to the East Coast Route and Swindon contains GWR items including the famous *City of Truro*.

As BR's officially approved preservation list contains far more locomotives than can possibly be displayed within the museum space available. Many of the locomotives are in store at Brighton awaiting restoration (an extremely costly item for which BR has no money available). Among these engines are *Lord Nelson*, *Sir Lamiel* (King Arthur), *Cheltenham* (Schools) and many others. BR has now been granted permission by Parliament to dispose of certain of these unwanted relics to other museums or organisations capable of restoring them and exhibiting them to the public. Some of them come under the heading 'Quick' rather than 'Dead' for some of the recipients have track on which to run the locomotives and they are actually steamed from time to time. Notable examples are the Britannia class Pacific 70013 *Oliver Cromwell* and the London, Tilbury & Southend 4-4-2 tank *Thundersley* at Alan Bloom's Bressingham Hall in Norfolk, together with one of the most famous of them all—*King George V* on semi-permanent loan to Bulmer's the cider people at Hereford. All these three engines are in excellent mechanical and external order. Others are to go to 7029 Clun Castle Ltd. at Tyseley.

Locomotives that can really be considered to be capable of working again (in the same way as the two GN Atlantics in 1953) would include the Midland Compound at Clapham and the GWR engines at Swindon. Let us hope that one day—perhaps if the Clapham Museum is actually moved up to the roundhouse at York—we may see some of them in steam again.

Not only have BR let some of their heirlooms go to private persons or companies, they have also distributed them to various municipal museums of transport or science and industry throughout the country. Some examples include 4073 *Caerphilly Castle* at the Science Museum at South Kensington, the LMS *City of Birmingham* in that City's Museum of Science and Industry, and six locomotives—the Midland 'Spinner' and 2-4-0, an LNWR G2 class 0-8-0, a Robinson 2-8-0, a Midland 4F 0-6-0 and the LNER's *Green Arrow* 2-6-2 at Leicester. Scotland has its own collection in the Glasgow Transport Museum.

During the later 1950s BR adopted a most enlightened practice of actually running some of its restored museum pieces from time to time on special trains. Due largely to the enthusiasm of Reggie Hanks, the then Chairman of the Western Region, *City of Truro* was fetched out of York Museum in 1957. She was given a thorough going over at Swindon and sent to Didcot shed where she was kept in normal service on light trains when not in use on specials. The following year the Midland Compound No 1000 was sent to Derby and completely overhauled. She was then repainted in Midland red and shedded in Derby roundhouse. Here she was treated with loving care—just like the Midland engines of yore—no mechanical coaling stage for her, it might have scratched the paint. Of all the restored engines, No 1000 was one of the most magnificent and it shows great credit that the Works and shed at Derby really did care.

Lastly there were the Scottish engines. These were the handiwork of the then General Manager of the Scottish Region, James Ness. There were four in all; the Caledonian single wheeler No 123, the North British *Glen Douglas*, the Highland Jones Goods 4-6-0 No 103 and the Great North of Scotland *Gordon Highlander*. All were overhauled and repainted in the old colours and put to work on specials. Normally they were shedded at Dawsholm, Glasgow, but they worked as far afield as Fort William and Kyle of Lochalsh. All in all the shed maintenance men and the loco crews adored them and it was a great morale booster. These engines are now retired to the Glasgow Corporation's Transport Museum but at least they had their fling.

The Spinner at Leicester (i) : During the Spring of 1968, the ex-Midland Railway 4-2-2 No 118 was hauled over to Leicester Museum and re-housed in her new home, an old tramway depot at Wigston

The Spinner at Derby: In prewar years, the MR loco No 118 was kept in the paint shop at Derby where this photograph was taken in 1936

The Spinner at Leicester (ii): A portrait taken from the cab of No 1A

Midland Engines at Leicester: The two ex-Midland
locomotives sit in their new home in April 1968

Shropshire & Montgomeryshire: The ancient *Gazelle* was taken out of service just after the Army took over the S&M in 1940. In June 1946 she was seen on display at Kinnerley, but has since been moved to Longmoor

Great Northern Lady: The famous Stirling single-wheeler No 1 is now in York Museum but in 1953 she was on display to the public at Doncaster Works

Waiting Renovation: Leicester Museum has also taken over the ex-LNER *Green Arrow,* an ex-GC ROD class 2-8-0, an ex-Midland class 4 0-6-0 and this LNWR Super D 0-8-0. They were moved to the old roundhouse for temporary safekeeping in the spring of 1968

C. M. Whitehouse

The last Coal Tank: In January 1958, BR closed the LNWR's tentacle into South Wales (via Abergavenny to Merthyr). The last train was worked by a Super D double headed to the sole surviving coal tank No 58926. This engine is now in the Industrial Railway Museum at Penrhyn Castle

Scottish Veteran (i) : The Jones' Goods stands on the turntable at Inverness in June 1960. She was being prepared to work the evening train to Kyle of Lochalsh

Scottish Veteran (ii) : The Caley Single No 123 was also brought out of retirement to work special trains. Along with the other veterans she was shedded at Dawsholm when this picture was taken in 1959

Scottish Veteran (iii): Once more the scene is Dawsholm in the same year. This time the loco is the ex-North British *Glen Douglas* complete with her brown livery and painted name

Scottish Veteran (iv): In her smart GNoS green livery *Gordon Highlander* (nicknamed The Soldier) leads *Glen Douglas* at Dawsholm in 1959. The engines have just come off a Glasgow special

City of Birmingham: This picture shows the last movements of 46235 on BR metals. Shortly after it was taken at Saltley the engine was moved by road to the Birmingham Museum of Science and Industry

Repton: No 926 is now over the water at Steamtown in the USA. She was restored at Eastleigh where this picture was was taken in 1967

Great Northern Atlantic: In the summer of 1953 Alan Pegler and his associates arranged for the removal of the two ex-GN Atlantics Nos 990 *Henry Oakley* and 251 from York Museum for limited excursion working. These pictures show the large boilered engine at Edge Hill shed Liverpool later in the year

On Shed Overseas: Canada and the USA

There was never a setting for steam which surpassed Canada. The endless oceans of prairie between the St Lawrence and the mountains or the trek through the forest country from Halifax to Montreal gave the traveller time to reflect. He could board his train, dine, read, and enjoy a full night's sleep—then rise again next morning to find what seemed to be the same inexhaustible 4-6-4 or 4-8-4 holding down the front end. The Canadians were tough but they knew how to look after their motive power, thinking nothing of despatching their relatively small rigid framed locomotives on to the grades of the Rockies and Selkirks that the Americans would not have dared to attempt without articulateds. But the snow capped peaks echoed back the thunder of the triple-headers which often resulted.

Both the CP and the CN were purists' delights for not only were their 4-6-4s and 4-8-4s classics in their own right but there were also other delightful pieces of machinery like the Pacifics which worked the fasts between Hamilton and Toronto on the Toronto, Hamilton & Buffalo, or those strange red 4-4-4s which worked up into the wilds towards Lake Huron. One could discover, too, the odd 2-8-0 tucked away for the night in a branch shed or a few 4-4-0s still at work in Nova Scotia.

We, who first saw the clear sharp outline of the New World from a troopship during World War II, came across the CN at Halifax. Here among the abundant food and the bright lights were the biggest steam engines that we had ever seen. They took us through snow and ice and frost and mountain to Moncton, NB, a railway town which acted as an RAF Reception Centre. Here, after we were inoculated and documented, we waited to be dispersed to training schools all over the northern part of the Continent. The CN was extremely kind to us and parties were regularly taken round the large divisional workshops and soon groups of railway enthusiasts would find their way to the station and running sheds. It was a good introduction, for the traffic was heavy and motive power ranged from the huge 4-8-4s and 4-8-2s down to light Pacifics and 0-8-0 'switchers'.

Later at Hamilton, Ontario, aquaintance was made with the CP as well. Indeed the Hamilton roundhouse was another ideal spot, for the line to Toronto was triple joint, Canadian Pacific, Canadian National and Toronto, Hamilton & Buffalo. We also saw locos off the New York Central including their famous Hudsons. The CP Pacifics in particular were superb machines and beautiful riders—a trip on the footplate at 70mph was almost like riding in a coach. The accompanying photographs taken at Hamilton were made with an old 116 Kodak Box camera lent to me by one of the signalmen who became a firm friend.

Time for hobbies was naturally in short supply but luckily I had been in correspondence for many years with a railwayman in Chicago. He was C. C. Orr, the depot master on the Illinois Central—a huge shed with over 200 engines—the line's motto emblazoned on a diamond device on some of the locos' tenders was 'Courtesy and Efficient Service Always'. Orr invited me to come down on leave to meet his family and his locomotives—an invitation gratefully accepted.

But it was Canadian steam which left its mark and two classes in particular. The CP dubbed its 4-6-4s Nos 2820-2864 'Royal Hudsons' and placed embossed crowns on their skirts. This was to commemorate No 2850 which hauled King George VI and Queen Elizabeth 3,100 miles without change on their 1937 tour of Canada. These were the Regal engines. The others were the CN's 4-8-4s. No admirer could call these Regal—Rugged would be the true description. No other word is quite so apt. The front end was almost overbearing with the fearsome looking Elesco feed water heater, the jutting number plates and centre headlight. There is still one left in service for enthusiasts' specials and I hope one day I can go back and admire her once again.

…adian Pacific
…These pleasant
…-2s were used
…ng the 1940s
…un the fast CP
…ices between
…milton and
…onto in Ontario.
…y had a good
…of speed and
…uently topped
…70s with very
…vy trains for
…r size. Hamilton
…d, 1943

Canadian Pacific (ii): This second picture of No 2216 was also taken on Hamilton shed in 1943. The engine was ready to take the evening fast to Toronto one Sunday evening in July

Canadian National: Moncton shed, New Brunswick was an ideal spot for the enthusiast in the 1940s. Not only did it house the big 4-8-4s and 4-8-2s, but these were often ex-Moncton work In October 1943, 4-6-2 No 6011 waits to off shed to pick up a train for St Johns, NB

Illinois Central (i): Chicago was the centre the IC and here at 27th Street were the shop No 2401, used for heavy passenger and fa freight work stands outside in October 1939

Illinois Central (ii): No 701 was a class 2-8-8-2. This class was mainly used on hea coal traffic in the more hilly areas. This pictu was taken at Tennessee in October 1939

Egypt, Palestine, Cyprus and India

Most of us who went to the Middle East between 1942 and 1945 either began or ended our sojourn at 22PTC Almaza on the outskirts of Cairo. Here, in the transit camp life was relatively free and most of us would go off into Cairo sometime during the day on the brown tram from Heliopolis. Fortunately for those who had an interest in railways the city tram terminus was adjacent to Cairo Main Station and close to the loco depot, and many happy hours were whiled away at both places. There was plenty to see for virtually everything was steam and the variety was fascinating.

Most of the expresses out of Cairo Main were worked by the Atlantics shedded at the local depot or Alexandria. Though outwardly similar in appearance these were supplied in batches from makers in the UK, Germany and USA over a period of 13 years from 1913 onwards. Some carried names and these were kept polished to perfection. Cairo shed also housed British, Belgian and German-built 2-6-0s, some ancient double-framed 0-6-0s, and some very good looking 4-4-0s built by North British as late as 1937, as well as the Robinson 2-8-0s of the WD, some doing their second spell of war service.

Strange as it may seem, thousands of miles from home and in the middle of a war, organised railway enthusiasm flourished in Cairo during those years. It is not known how many railway enthusiasts visited the Middle East during the course of their military service but of those who did a hard core set up a branch of the Railway Correspondence and Travel Society. This met at 'Music for All', Sharia Maruf and preserved in the land of the Nile the prewar Friday club night traditions of the Society enabling many members to meet and pursue their interests in both home and Middle East railways. Many excursions of railway interest were organised and there must be little doubt that this helped considerably to alleviate the monotony of continual exile for those lucky enough to be even temporarily base posted. Truth is sometimes stranger than fiction.

The other place of interest in Cairo was the Railway Museum which was in fact an annexe to Cairo Main Station. The exhibits here included a quaint 2-2-4 combined engine and saloon built for the personal use of Said Pasha, Viceroy of Egypt, by Robert Stephenson and Company in 1867. This contraption was restored to museum condition in that its nearside (only) had an intricate ornate painted design on it. There was also a further Robert Stephenson loco in the form of an 1867 double framed 0-6-0 and many other small exhibits including models.

Some of us also went further east to the Italian Hospital, Jerusalem. We got there by means of the swing bridge over the Suez Canal at El Kantara. This part of the Middle East was then known as Palestine and the PR had some interesting motive power of its own. There were still some of the 1918 Baldwin 4-6-0s in service and six had returned from a visit to Armstrong Whitworth's at Newcastle as 4-6-2 tanks. These and the 4-6-4 tanks converted in the PR's own workshops in 1937 were used on the Jerusalem branch from Lydda along with some British-built 2-8-4 tanks. Lydda was not only a junction but a jumping off point for a large RAF airfield. It also had a large shed containing the classes mentioned above plus the odd Stanier 2-8-0 or wartime American 2-8-2 for the main line fasts to Cairo.

Further north from Lydda lay Haifa, and from here the PR was extended over a new standard-gauge main line in 1943 to Beirut and Tripoli thus making a connection with the Syrian system known as the Damas, Hamah et Prolonguements, better known as the DHP. Haifa was also the jumping off place for the 'Eolo'—a bug-ridden ferry running to Famagusta in Cyprus where one came upon the unique 2ft 6in-gauge system. But that is another story.

Cairo Main (i): The depot for main line work was only a few hundred yards from Cairo Main Station. It housed a variety of engines (all oil burners), from the graceful Atlantics to British-built ROD 2-8-0s. Here in May 1945, a 2-6-0 fuels up from the oil tanks. In the background is the 4-4-2 used for royal trains, No 56 *King Fouad I*

Cairo Main (ii): Also on the shed in 1945 were some NBL 4-4-0s used for light passenger work. This is No 254, painted in apple green livery and looking very smart

Cairo Main (iii): These double framed 0-6-0s of 1899 vintage were generally used for shunting work, but occasionally helped out on some of the locals on the Suez line. This is a shed pilot in May 1945

North Western at Karachi: This inside cylinder 2-6-4 tank
of the then NWR of India was photographed on Karachi
shed in March 1946

Nicosia Shed: The Cyprus Government Railway was narrow gauge (2ft 6in) and most of its
passenger services were railcar worked. This 2-6-2 tank was photographed in April 1943

Palestine, Lydda (i): These 4-6-2 tanks were rebuilds
of earlier Baldwin 4-6-0s. No 8 was used on the Lydda–
Jerusalem line in 1943

Palestine, Lydda (ii): The ubiquitous Stanier 8F 2-8-0s were found all over the Middle East
during the war. By the middle '40s they were working some of the through Cairo–Haifa trains via
El Kantara. No 70305 was waiting to go out to Cairo early one morning in March 1943

France

The ship of steam is sinking in France as elsewhere, but in happy contrast to the way it has gone down in other countries the flag is still flying at the masthead. Those steam-hauled services which operated in 1968 and to date, in the early part of 1969, were headed by locomotives well cared for mechanically and still masters of their jobs, whether emanating from the Calais depot of M. Lavieville or Nevers or Nantes. The final year of the express engines proper on the SNCF was 1968—it saw out the regular workings of the heavy Mountain type 241Ps on the Paris-Clermont trains and January 1969 brought the diesels to Calais replacing the few remaining 231Ks on the 'Flèche d'Or' and other expresses. There may well have been the rearguard of a once proud army, but at least they were treated as such.

The French used Pacifics a great deal and indeed this was once the normal wheel arrangement for express and *rapide* workings. The 4-8-2s were less numerous, working mainly on the Est and the Paris-Lyon-Mediterranean systems based on such sheds as Chaumont and Nevers, although in the mid-1950s some went to Brittany. In addition the 4-6-2 with a rather lower axle load was normally allowed to run about 10 per cent faster. Many of these engines had been rejuvenated by re-building during the 1930s and 1940s with improved steam passages and valves, and high degree superheat.

The classic example here was a rather unremarkable series of Pacifics built for the Paris-Orleans Railway Company in 1909, transformed in 1929 under the direction of André Chapelon into the later SNCF class 231E with an increase in power from 2,100 to 3,500hp. These machines were concentrated on the Nord Region and their final days were spent working on the Amiens-Calais section until April 10, 1967, when 231E21 made her final journey working to the last on the 'Flèche d'Or'. She has now gone to Switzerland for preservation.

In the early 1960s the Calais stud of Pacifics began to be augmented by 231Ks, rebuilt from the original PLM class C of 1912, and these were the engines which survived on the boat trains until January 8, 1969. The Ks thought nothing of taking 530 tons on the Calais-Amiens trains.

The other French Pacifics well in evidence up to a year previously were the État 231Ds based mainly at Le Havre and Paris (Batignolles) for working the *rapides* and Ocean Specials. Some of these engines were still working out of Nantes as late as the spring of 1968.

Today if one visits a SNCF steam depot the main inmates will almost certainly be the American or Canadian-built 141Rs—a French equivalent of the LMS 'Black Fives'. Some 1,340 of these 2-8-2s were hurriedly designed and built shortly after the war in an attempt to make up the critical shortage of motive power. As far as general European standards go these are not particularly big engines, but slightly larger than their native contemporaries of class 141P. They are of typically American design, rugged and simple, but with a healthy appetite for coal since they follow the American principle of 'ease of maintenance first'. Very few modifications were required by the French, one of them being the provision of rakish smoke deflectors. The 141Rs have rendered yeoman service and comprised over two-thirds of the last thousand active SNCF steam engines. Three hundred were originally equipped to burn oil and a further 320 were converted after arrival in France. The last French-designed 2-8-2s, the 141Ps, were compounds and although these were more complicated machines the saving in fuel and sounder engineering made possible by better balancing made the relationship between the American 141R and the French 141P akin to that between a Ford and a Rolls-Royce.

But now the variety has gone and on passenger work at least the diesel reigns supreme on non-electrified lines, apart at the present from reliefs and the slower trains out of places such as Calais. There are at the time of writing some odd 241Ps at Chaumont, Nevers and Le Mans but they cannot last for long. The French steam depots (and there is still a fair number) will house mainly the mixed traffic 141R plus a few 2-8-0s and odd varieties of tank engine. In spite of this, steam is still to be seen in unlikely places (Paris Nord, for example) and it is worth seeking out for it has not long to go.

Quimper: The West Brittany line had steam up till 1967.
In 1964 there were still 4-8-2s in regular service on the
Paris expresses, but the mainstay of all SNCF services
were (and still are) the American- and Canadian-built
141Rs.   Here is No 1118 coming off the turntable in
September

Rennes (i) (ii): In its
last years this depot
housed the D class
Pacifics, 141Rs and
the compound 141Ps
which were used on
most passenger trains.
These two pictures
show 141P 225 in
September 1964

Rennes (iii): 141P
210 gets up steam
outside the depot on a
September morning in
1964

Rennes (iv): D Class Pacific No 732 waits for a Paris-bound train in September 1964

Calais (i): One of the most famous of all French engines. 231E class Pacific No 23 waits on the shed in August 1966. She had just come off the 'Fleche d'Or' from Paris

Nantes: Still one of the largest steam sheds in France, in August 1967, apart from the 141Rs (759 shown here), there were 241Ps and 281Ds plus various freight locomotives

Calais (ii): These 230Ds worked the locals out of Calais up to the mid-1960s. No 12 was photographed on shed in August 1965

Turkey, Istanbul West and East

Coming in to Turkey by the 'Direct Orient Express' (after all, the *only* proper way of doing it) you cross the border from Greece in the hours of darkness and it is not until breakfast time that it becomes apparent that the train is steam-hauled once more—almost certainly by either an ex-German 52 class 2-10-0 lent by the Germans during World War II and still in service, or by one of those ubiquitous machines double headed by one of eighteen light 2-8-0s built by Batignolles in 1925. These engines will almost certainly have come from Halkali depot situated a little way outside Istanbul at the end of the 50 cycle monophase ac electrification running out of Sirkeci terminus, to which point steam no longer runs. Halkali depot lies close to the seashore, surrounded by a stockade, and houses the lighter axle load engines used in Western Turkey.

The other shed at Istanbul is across the Bosphorous at Haydarpasa—now mainly a diesel depot, for the Ankara expresses are now either diesel multiple units or hauled by American-supplied main line diesel locomotives. There are, however, still some steam locomotives here, including the Henschel-built 4-6-4 tanks (similar to the Prussian T18 class) seen on the suburban services and some 4-8-0s by the same firm used mainly on freight working. On trip-goods trains, as they are small engines in comparison, one can even now come across an LMS Stanier 2-8-0 transferred from lines further east. Haydarpasa was in a state of rebuilding when I last visited the shed in October 1966—the steelwork for the new diesel depot was well in hand and almost ready for its dedication ceremony. I discovered this by accident for each time I went round the shed I noticed a large, very tame sheep tethered to one of the stanchions. On enquiry as to why the animal was there, apparently well cared for, I was told that on the completion of the shell it would be slaughtered and its blood spilt on the floor as a token of good luck—a sort of Turkish topping out ceremony.

Steam in Turkey is, as everywhere else, on the retreat, but eastwards beyond Ankara it is still in full force. There are German-built 2-8-2s and 2-10-0s, far larger than the utility 52 class 'Kriegsloks' and embodying such refinements as Riggenbach counter pressure braking. Some very handsome Robert Stephenson-built 2-8-2s of 1929 vintage and Baldwin-built Ministry of Supply 2-8-2s all based on Izmir, and further east steam reigns almost supreme. So there is much to be seen yet.

Halkali Shed (i) & (ii): This is the steam depot on the western outskirts of Istanbul. It provides the locomotives for all the through services from Istanbul to Western Europe including the 'Direct Orient Express.' These pictures show one of the ex-German 2-10-0s borrowed during the war; they were taken in October 1966

Halkali Shed (iii): A German-built
4-8-0 receives fitters' attention in
October 1966

Halkali Shed (iv): An ex-German Federal
Railways' 2-10-0 and a 0-8-0 stand inside the
stockade in October 1966

Halkali Shed (v): A French-built 4-8-0 used
mainly on the western passenger services sits
on the shed also in October 1966

Haydarpassa (i) : The German built 4-8-0s were used to run the long distance suburban trains out of Haydarpassa—the terminus on the Asian side of Istanbul. This and the other pictures on these two pages were taken in October 1966

Haydarpassa (ii) : The 4-6-4 tanks of German origin worked the normal suburban trains for many years. During the building of the new depot in 1966/7 they were housed in a temporary structure for maintenance purposes

Haydarpassa (iii) : An 0-8-0 shunter fitted with a snow plough simmers outside the shed in the early evening

Yugoslavia

As Yugoslavia is still a comparatively new country, having been formed after World War I from Serbia, Bosnia and Herzegovina, Montenegro and parts of Austria and Hungary, its locomotive stock is varied and interesting. Steam is distributed fairly widely over the country but the principal express services are in the main diesel-hauled by General Motors' machines, one exception being the 'Direct Orient Express' between Nis and the Bulgarian border.

To many visitors who arrive by rail, Ljubljana is the first large town to be encountered. This section of line was originally part of the old Austrian Sudbahn main line from Vienna to Trieste. There is still a steam shed here though its inhabitants are far less numerous than they were even in 1966, but they include some ex-Austrian 0-10-0s with poppet valves and Borsig two-cylinder mixed-traffic 2-8-2s supplied to the Yugoslav Railways in 1930. The shed can easily be seen from the station platforms and there is nearly always something on the move. Zagreb is a quite busy spot for steam though once again mainly on freight workings and here one comes across locos from the old Serbian State Railways in the form of the O1 class 2-6-2s and some ex-Hungarian 4-8-0s and 2-6-2s.

Belgrade is another good spot and the depot here contains a fair variety of locomotives. On shed in August 1968 were ex-German 52 class 'Kriegslok' 2-10-0s (JZ class 33), ex-Serbian O1s, standard JZ O5 class Pacifics, and former Hungarian 342 class 2-6-2 tanks. In addition there were also several of the ubiquitous ex-US Army 0-6-0 tanks, some of which were built to the same design in recent years at Slavonski Brod. For the record, these Yugoslav-built American engines were modified considerably, the principal difference being the use of plate instead of bar frames. The cabs have also been rather improved and these engines have taller chimneys and flatter tops to their domes and sandboxes than their American sisters. Other locomotives supplied from overseas included Vulcan Foundry 2-8-0s.

The shed at Belgrade is well worth a visit for the staff there are keen and anxious to be of all help possible (provided of course that you have the necessary authority to make the visit). The goings on around the shed and most of the yard movements can be watched from a footbridge that joins the shed to the main road (served frequently by trams from the City centre).

Getting up Steam: An ex-Hungarian 2-6-2 tank, a Yugoslav 05 class Pacific and a 2-6-2—both German built—raise steam one morning in August 1968. All the Belgrade photographs were taken at this time

Wartime Engines: Baldwin design 0-6-0 tank (originally an UNRRA class) and an ex-German 2-10-0 make interesting contrasts. Some of these 0-6-0 tanks were built under American licence at Slavonski Brod in 1958

05 Pacific (i) & (ii): These engines, designed in the 1930s, are now largely relegated to secondary trains by American-built diesels. They still work express services towards the Bulgarian border and most are kept in excellent internal and external condition. Note the Yugoslav flag on the smoke deflectors

UNRRA Engine: The bulk of the Vulcan Foundry's Liberation 2-8-0s went to the JDZ. They are classified as 38, this representative being No 38 015

Serbian Engine: The 01 class 2-6-2s were Yugoslavia's first standard class. The design dates from 1912 and is four-cylindered. They are now mainly used on local services

Morning Duties: 01 class 2-6-2, 05 class Pacific and 38 class 2-8-0

Hungary and Austria

Although it may seem a little strange in this day and age to lump these two countries together, it is still well within living memory that the Austro-Hungarian Empire was in full sway; and remember too, that in spite of a long wait at the border it is still only a morning's journey from Budapest to Vienna.

Today the trains running between the two capitals are hauled by electric locomotives, but adjacent to the two termini there are steam locomotive depots and steam engines still run in and out of Budapest East and Vienna East. The engines in both depots will be mechanically superb, but those at Budapest will be clean whilst the Austrian engines rarely if ever see a cleaner's rag. In both countries there is only a small number of classes, for Hungary has standardised thoroughly and Austria is running down its steam fast.

As one would expect, it is not easy for enthusiasts from western Europe to obtain permission to photograph railway subjects in Hungary but it *can* be obtained, usually for one place only—generally speaking it is granted more frequently in Budapest than in the country areas. Austria on the other hand is much more free and easy, permission is granted freely and as in England photography is no problem when carried out in places usually accessible to the public.

In Hungary most of the larger depots contain a supply of the mixed traffic 424 class 4-8-0s introduced in 1927, and these are used indiscriminately on fast passenger workings and heavy freights. There are also numbers of 2-6-2s of class 324 in evidence—this light design handles most of the secondary main line work at the present time although the MAV still has a few of its rakish 4-6-0s of class 327 in service. Until recently the Hungarian tank locomotives were perhaps best known by the 242 class introduced in 1936/9. There were four of these odd looking streamlined 4-4-4s and they were used on the Budapest-Misholc trains—two of these engines double headed on the 'Baltic-Orient Express' was quite something to see. For general branch line services there are three classes of 2-6-2 tank, including the ultra lightweight 376 class used on lines laid with light rail such as that at Siofok close to the shores of that popular holiday resort at Lake Balaton.

The Austrian engines are headed by the German 52 class 2-10-0 and wherever steam is to be found in that country there is almost certainly one of these engines nearby; there are two varieties—with and without the Giesl ejector. Another fairly numerous class is the 77 class 4-6-2 tank, used mainly on suburban services when these are steam hauled—for example some of the trains in and out of Vienna East. There are three sheds in Vienna containing steam locomotives—Ost, Nord (Prater) and Franz Joseph—the latter contains some locomotives destined for the transport museum and a delightful little 2-2-2 tank—this is No 69.02 and is used for bridge testing. Other locomotive classes to be found in Austria include the 392 class 0-8-0 tanks used for shunting work, which have many interchangeable parts with the 93 class 2-8-2 tanks, in service on some of the hillier branches like that to Puchberg. Many of these tank engines are also fitted with the Giesl oblong ejector which reduces back pressure and increases the efficiency of draughting, thus improving performance.

Budapest East: An array of clean 424 class 4-8-0s sitting outside the depot in June 1967

Siofok: These small 275 class 2-6-2 tanks are used on the lesser branch services. No 038 waits for water at this small junction shed, alongside Lake Balaton, in June 1967

Vienna, Franz Joseph: This shed has no normal steam allocation but is used to store some locomotives destined for the technical museum. It is also the home of this rather odd 2-2-2 tank which was photographed in June 1967

Vienna, Prater: These 4-6-2 tanks of class 77 (all Giesl fitted) still run some of the suburban trains out of here and Vienna Ost. With their almost silent exhausts and total absence of knock, they run like the proverbial sewing machine

Vienna, Ost: This shed, just beyond the Sud/Ost station, houses
mainly 52 class ex-German 2-10-0s of both Giesl and pre-Giesl
appearance. There are also a few 77 class 4-6-2 tanks and 0-8-0
shunters, plus one or two locomotives destined for preservation

Finland

This is the land of lakes and forests, saunas and reindeer but above all of woodburning steam. True, most of the wood-burners have retreated north and north east and they are in the main limited to station pilot work but they are, in early 1969, still there. Most of the more northerly sheds have at least one Tk-3 on their strength—sometimes the only steam engine at all—these include Oulu, where there is also a repair shop, Kemi and Rovaniemi close to the Arctic Circle. Like all the VR engines these 2-8-0s are well kept and mechanically sound. They make a grand sight whilst standing alongside those charming wooden scenic railway-type fuelling stages which adorn most sheds, or for example at Rovaniemi, standing at the head of a train of the large wooden sleeping cars for the Helsinki express.

Steam is spread fairly widely over Finland and most sheds have a small allocation. There is little at Helsinki itself although there are still one or two Pacifics—most of the steam is in the east of the country. Riihimaki an hour's journey out of Helsinki has a fair sprinkling of Pacifics, Mikados, 2-8-2 tanks and rows of very dead 4-6-0s and American 2-10-0s. Kouvola, where the line to Russia via Vainikkala branches off is a very good centre. Here is the home of three of the heavy 0-10-0 tanks of class Vr-3; these have boilers, cylinders and motion interchangeable with the Pr-1 class 2-8-2 tanks and are used for work in the Kouvola hump yard. This yard is busy night and day and to see one of these powerful engines pushing a heavy train of Russian bogie wagons, whose couplings are completely rigid and unsprung, over the hump is worth the price of the air ticket; the soft brown Russian coal gives smoke effects equal to any and puts the old Lickey bankers in the shade.

Finnish steam could well be with us, though scattered, until some years into the 1970s—it is unusual in that it is the standard Russian gauge of 5ft 0in and that it has locomotives fitted with cow catchers and air operated bells for use in the vicinity of stations and goods yards. Visitors (obtaining prior permission, which is easy) are extremely welcome—the VR even going to the length of encouraging tourists to visit its installations and to take photographs of them. Naturally the Authorities are proudest of their several achievements in the world of electrification, diesel haulage and really excellent rolling stock, but here steam is not a dirty word and the enthusiast is welcome. This, then, is a fitting point to end this volume.

Wood Burner: 2-8-0 No 1150 is a member of class TK-3 built between 1928 and 1950 in Finland and Denmark. In the autumn of 1968, she was shedded at Roveniemi and used mainly for station pilot work. She is one of the Danish-built engines

Fuelling Shed: Most of the depots on the Vr (Finnish State Railways) possess these interesting switchback-type fuelling points for their wood business. The fuel is birch wood in logs 2ft 6in long and is transported to the tipping point in narrow gauge containers

Finnish Mikado: Tr-1 class 2-8-2 No 1049 is serviced at Riihimaki shed before picking up a northbound troop train in September 1968

Tanks at Riihimaki: The Pr-1 class 2-8-2 tanks were used regularly on the Helsinki locals until the coming of the diesels. No 770 waits as standby loco alongside Vr-5 class 0-6-2 tank on a sunny morning in September 1968